D0061890

Talking Dogs

SAM MASON

Inspiring Voices®
A Service of Guideposts

ISBN: 978-1-4624-0098-0 (sc)
ISBN: 978-1-4624-0097-3 (e)

Library of Congress Control Number: 2012935600

Inspiring Voices books may be ordered through booksellers or by contacting:

Inspiring Voices
1663 Liberty Drive
Bloomington, IN 47403
www.inspiringvoices.com
1-(866) 697-5313

Printed in the United States of America

Inspiring Voices rev. date: 03/27/2012

Contents

Acknowledgements

I want to recognize some special people who contributed to the writing of this book. Three in particular agreed to proof-read and critique my work. They helped me hone earlier drafts and correct some typos and grammatical errors. They also complimented and encouraged me in this project.

My appreciation goes out to my wife of 41 years, the love of my life: Carol; my pastor, a true man of God: Dr. Darrell Waller; and my good friend and fellow writer: Linda Jary. Their involvement resulted in a better final product. May God bless them for their kindness!

Of course, the chief recipient of my thanks is the Lord Himself. To Him I owe my life and whatever gifts He's allowed me to use to advance His Kingdom. It was, after all, Him who blessed me with my pets, and used them to favor me with the spiritual insights shared in this book. To God be the glory!

Introduction

I confess to being an animal lover. There's a good chance you are too, since you picked up this book. There's no doubt that my love of animals in general, and of dogs in particular, has cast a powerful influence on the thoughts contained herein.

Yet I'm equally convinced that the hand of God has also been at work. He's never uninvolved in any aspect of the lives of His children. He's frequently the unseen director behind the stage curtain. I suspect He ordained my canine relationships, though I cannot say for certain. But I'm sure He's used my beloved pets to speak to me.

Throughout the Bible the Lord employs His creation to communicate His truths to open hearts. Animals become living illustrations of those truths. In the Old Testament God declared that those who trust in Him will "soar on wings like eagles" (Isaiah 40:31). He asserted that conies (small short-eared burrowing mammals) are examples of wisdom, because although they have little strength, they're smart enough to make their homes in the crags of the rocks (Proverbs 30:26). He related the swiftly running deer's thirst for water to our soul's thirst for Him (Psalm 42:1).

In the New Testament Jesus commissioned His disciples with a warning to be "as shrewd as snakes and as innocent as doves" (Matthew 10:16). He illustrated His Father's care for people through His concern for tiny sparrows (Luke 12:6). Christ Himself had compassion on a spiritually and physically hungry crowd because the Bible says he saw them as being "like sheep without a shepherd" (Mark 6:34). He healed the daughter of a desperate Canaanite woman, when that mother compared her offspring to the little dogs who "eat the crumbs that fall from their master's table" (Matthew 15:27).

These are but a few examples of how the Lord teaches us life principles through the lives of His creatures. Of course, all such examples have their limitations. The natural world is an imperfect reflection of the Kingdom of God. Still, it *is* a reflection. As such, the Lord repeatedly uses the *natural* as a means of expanding our understanding of the *spiritual*.

In the 22nd chapter of the book of Numbers we're told how God even supernaturally enabled speech from the mouth of a donkey in order to communicate to a wayward prophet. Now, my hounds have never spoken English. Yet over the years I have heard the Lord talk to my spirit through the lives of the dogs my wife and I have been blessed to own and love.

I'm no expert on canine behavior. But I have done some research on the subject, and as with any reasonably intelligent person, I'm capable of making rational deductions from extended observation. As a consequence, I've become quite confident of a few simple conclusions about their nature.

You may ask "why is this book about talking *dogs*?" "Why not cats, birds, or chimpanzees, for example?" The first and most obvious reason is that I've had far more experience with this species than any other. Still, there are other rationale.

So why allow dogs to be a "stand-in" for God's children in certain analogies to our relationship with Him? One reason is canine intelligence. But that alone is not enough. There may be animals of greater intelligence. I think the key is that among creatures of higher intellect, none has more wide-spread intimate social interaction with their human masters than dogs.

Numerous features of canine dealings with people can characterize our relationship with the Lord. Dogs have an inherent recognition of the chain of command. Once they've acknowledged an authority figure, also known as the alpha dog or pack leader, they become attached. They take pleasure in being around that person, and are capable of giving and receiving great affection. These, among other distinctives, make dogs easy illustrations of certain spiritual principles.

Many characteristics of "man's best friend" are common to the entire species. Others are somewhat peculiar to certain breeds. Still other character traits are unique to individual dogs. Whatever their origin, most of these canine qualities have easy parallels among humans. That's what makes the information in this book useful.

In the accounts that follow, at times you'll see me (as master of my canine friends) representing God in these allegories. That, of course, is clearly a far from perfect comparison, but a useful one nonetheless. My pets then, represent us as God's children. That, too, is in many ways a poor correlation, yet probably a much better one than the first. Each chapter in this book deals with a spiritual truth wonderfully illustrated through the lives of my pets.

The only claim to divine validity these lessons from my "talking dogs" can make, is that which flows from the Holy Spirit's inspiration of these insights, and their consistency with the Word of God. I believe there is a stream of both coursing through this book or I would not have written it. My prayer is that it will help you better understand your Heavenly Master and your relationship with Him.

Chapter 1:
Imparted Value

*Deuteronomy 14:2 - "...the Lord has chosen
you to be his treasured possession."*

ALL OF OUR DOGS have been special to me. I've cared about them quite deeply. One day I began to think about this and asked myself the question, "What gives them such value to me?" They're of no *practical* use. Grant you now, some dogs do have useful value. Watch dogs, guard dogs, police dogs, seeing eye dogs, etc., fall into that category. Mine, however, have performed none of those functions. From a *practical* standpoint they've only been a drain on our resources. Yet I've treasured them. Why?

I realized that simply put, what gives my pets worth is my love for them. I *chose* them. Intellectually they're inferior to me. Still, I love them and consider them cherished objects of my affection.

Do they love me back? I guess it depends on your interpretation of love. Most experts say animals are not capable of love in the human sense. Yet dogs do have the capacity for some kind of strong attachment to their masters. Whether it's actually love or not, we draw much satisfaction from it.

What do you cherish most in life... possessions, achievements, pleasures? The Bible teaches us that the highest valued things in life ought to be *relationships*. Our most fulfilling experiences are those that flow out of healthy, godly relationships. The Great Designer set it up that way. And *God's kind of relationships* are always based on *God's kind of love*.

I Corinthians 13 is often referred to as the *love chapter.* It identifies love as "the most excellent way." It then goes on to catalog the characteristics of that purest of emotions. But I'd have to nominate I John as the *love book.* In that five chapter epistle, the word occurs twenty-six times. The focal point of all the beloved apostle's discussion on the subject is encapsulated in this three word statement: "God is love" (I John 4:16). All true love on the planet must trace to its ultimate source: the heart of God. It's Who He is... and it's why relationships exist.

The Lord has no needs as we understand needs. What can I possibly do that will add anything to the omnipotent Sovereign of the universe? He's entirely self-sufficient. In and of myself I have nothing useful to offer Him. As a matter of record, my life should have brought Him more disappointment than delight.

Yet His love nature desires a recipient. That, I believe, is the moving force behind creation in general, and the making of people in particular. God made humanity in His own image (Genesis 1:26) in order to lavish His love on us. This fellowship of love between God and people is the model for all other relationships.

When in the Garden of Eden mankind chose pride over God's love, we forfeited that wonderfully intimate fellowship with our Creator. Yet His great love had already determined to pay the price necessary for reconciliation... a price that no mere mortal could pay. You know the story. John 3:16 - "For God so loved the world that he gave his one and only Son, that whoever believes in him shall not perish but have eternal life."

Human beings have immense value *not* because of what we can do for our adoptive (Ephesians 1:5) Heavenly Father. We're his "treasured possession" *simply because He loves us.* We would not even be capable of loving God if He hadn't first loved us. I John 4:19 emphasizes this fundamental fact. "We love because he first loved us."

Can we choose to love God? The answer is a resounding "Yes!" That's the most important determination we'll ever make for all eternity. But we could never have chosen Him, if He had not made the primal decision to choose us.

We may rightly bask in in His amazing love, but we have no right to take pride in being its object. It's not something we've earned. The reality declared in Ephesians 2:8,9 eliminates any possibility of pride in connection with our reconciliation to God through His Son. "For it is by grace you have been saved, through faith — and this not from yourselves, it is the gift of God — not by works, so that no one can boast."

God's redemptive love is transformational. It pardons a seditious rebel from the death sentence. It takes a fallen creature and raises it to the position of a prized son or daughter of the King. His love regenerates itself in the soul of a once self-absorbed creature, turning that person into an expression of God's love to others in need. No other force in the universe can accomplish what the love of God can!

All of our dogs were deliberately chosen by us. Most of them were rescued from rejection... sometimes even death. They were adopted into our family. We didn't pick them because they could be of service to us. We chose them because our love sought a beneficiary. And our love... even tender affection toward an animal... is a reflection of that of our Maker.

My dogs are incapable of knowing just how much I love them. Their limited intelligence restricts their comprehension of human love. So it is with our inability to fully grasp the breadth and depth of God's love for us. But the powerful fact remains: *God is love.* That's what imparts value to each and every one of us.

Chapter 2:
Seek His Face

Psalm 27:8 - "My heart says of you, seek his face! Your face, Lord, I will seek."

SOMETIMES IT AMAZES ME how a Scripture passage I've read innumerable times can suddenly spring to life with new meaning. One such occasion was when Ranger, our eleven pound Italian Greyhound, was sitting on my lap as I relaxed on the recliner.

I can't say where my mind had been at the instant of inspiration. Was I praying or meditating, or were my thoughts far from things divine? Spiritual insight doesn't always arrive in moments or by means we might expect.

I noticed that familiar endearing little tilt of the head as he looked me directly in the face. I found myself wondering what his purpose was. A second later I warmed to the sublime pleasure of divine inspiration, as the explanation flowed into my stream of thoughts. Ranger was seeking my face!

You see, dogs become students of their human owners. They need to understand their masters in order to better respond to them. Their comprehension of spoken human language is limited to a relative handful of words. Their capacity to understand a creature of far greater intellect is restricted. So they study our movements: facial expressions, hand gestures, and other body language. They can't possibly know everything we know, but they labor to understand us as best they can, to please us, and to gain our favor. I recognize those limitations in my canine companions, and appreciate their efforts. In fact, those efforts draw more love from me.

4

That's a useful parallel for better grasping our relationship with the Lord.

Like dogs, we have limited understanding of our Master. That limitation may cause us to make the mistake God refers to in Psalm 50:21 when He declares: "… you thought I was altogether like you." He's not! In Isaiah 55:8,9 we hear Him expand on that difference. "'For my thoughts are not your thoughts, neither are my ways your ways,' declares the LORD. 'As the heavens are higher than the earth, so are my ways higher than your ways and my thoughts than your thoughts.'"

He's infinite. We're finite. He sees everything. We see "but a poor reflection" (I Corinthians 13:12). So how do we "seek the face" of someone who is so far our superior? God understands our weakness and He's provided a means for us to get to know Him better in spite of our limitations. In a sense He came down to our level.

The Lord reveals Himself through His Word. That's where our pursuit begins. Through human instruments such as prophets and apostles He gave us His *written Word*: the Bible. Then through sending His Son to earth He gave us the *Word in flesh*: Jesus. So we read the Scriptures, and through them also discover Jesus. There we begin to glimpse the face of God.

How sad that too few professing Christians read and study the Bible on any regular basis. In fact, studies indicate that fewer than one in ten has ever even read the entire book once! Do you want to seek the face of the Lord? Do you want to know Him better? Start by developing a daily habit of reading the Bible. In the verse that opens this chapter, the psalmist's heart demands he seek the face of God. He responds to that heart cry with a powerful "I will!" If you, too, hear that call, begin your search with the Word of God.

But beyond the Scriptures there are other ways to seek God's face. Like the devoted canine who carefully considers his human master's movements, we can learn much from observing how the Lord works. Pay attention to the ways of God as the Holy Spirit moves upon hearts during church services. Learn from His interventions in your life and those of your fellow believers. Behind His *works* are

His *ways*. Determine to become a student of the Master at every opportunity.

In other places in Scripture we're encouraged to seek God's dwelling place (Deuteronomy 12:5), His counsel (I Kings 22:5), and His help (II Chronicles 20:4). Those are all godly pursuits. Yet seeking God's *face* extends our quest to a deeper level of intimacy. The "face" speaks of who a person is. It ultimately reveals the depths of one's character. The person who seeks the face of the Lord reaches past where He is, what He does, and what He says. They're responding to the human's deepest yearning for divine encounter.

Here's where, like the psalmist, we "gaze upon the beauty of the Lord" (Psalm 27:4). This is what the Apostle Paul anticipates in its final form when the "poor reflection" we now view, yields to eternity's "face to face" uninhibited knowledge of God (I Corinthians 13:12). Only then will it produce its *fullness*. Still, in this realm of time, seeking the face of the Lord rewards it practitioners with rich benefits.

Seeking His face does not happen easily in the rush of modern western life. We need to set aside the day's business for a while. And, as with Ranger, we must abide in the Master's Presence, focusing on understanding what the expressions of His face may reveal. Maybe this is the spiritual equivalent of what's commonly referred to in today's vernacular as "face time." Whether assembling with our brothers and sisters in the Lord, or spending time alone in our "closet" or "room" (Matthew 6:6), we encounter God in an intimate way.

Often seeking the face of God involves patience or persistence. Sometimes it even includes pain. That was the case with Jacob in Genesis chapter 32. It was a pivotal moment in his life. He was returning to the land the Lord had promised to him, his father, and his grandfather. He'd sent his family and servants on ahead, and was alone in the darkness. Or so he thought…

In the evening of his supposed solitude he encountered a man… a *man* who turned out to be *God in flesh*. For what was likely hours Jacob wrestled with this powerful being. His weary muscles ached from the unrelenting tension. Then came the excruciating pain that tore through his body when "his hip was wrenched" (verse 25). Yet Jacob refused to give up until he experienced the blessing he desired.

His reward? He gained a changed name and a changed nature. Jacob, "the trickster," became Israel, "a prince with God." The man who did things *his* way began the transformation into the man who did things *God's* way. The name Jacob gave that place reveals what had happened on that sacred ground. "Peniel" literally means "the face of God."

The noblest motivation for every child of God is pleasing Him. In doing so we'll enjoy His favor. How much do you want to please Him? How intensely do you desire to walk in His favor? How thirsty are you for "face time" with the Lord? Are you willing to set aside one-on-one time with the Master, learning to discern His subtlest expressions? Will you even persevere through pain?

Let's learn how to seek His face. The highest prize of that discipline will be a deepening experience of His love and truth in our lives... the rich treasure of a growing intimacy with our Heavenly Father!

Chapter 3:
The Wisdom and Beauty of a Submissive Spirit

James 3:17 - "But the wisdom that comes from heaven is... submissive..."

I Peter 3:4 - "...the unfading beauty of a gentle and quiet spirit..."

SHE WAS THE MOST beautiful dog we'd ever owned. What fabulous breed was this gorgeous canine? She was a mutt! We adopted her from the S.P.C.A. shelter, and they weren't even sure what breeds might be in her bloodline. Their best guess was collie, shepherd, and maybe some beagle. No exotic purebred was "Tippy."

Oh, by the way, she was named Tippy by the folks at the shelter because she was missing the tip of one ear. Not exactly championship show dog material. But she *was* beautiful. And that beauty was more than fur deep. Tippy was the most beautiful dog we ever owned because she had the most loving, submissive spirit. Her predominant desire was to please us.

Twenty-first century American culture glorifies ego. Our pop heroes are generally not self-sacrificing nor self-deprecating. They're more likely to be self-satisfying and self-promoting. They exalt themselves. And we, the American public, worship them. If at all possible, we even emulate them. Those who cannot or will not follow their arrogant example are usually considered wimps who'll be despised and trampled under the advance of the forceful.

Unfortunately, much of this wicked culture has been embraced by the church. However, this strong willed "me first" philosophy is the antithesis of the lifestyle to which God calls His people. It's perverse *worldly* wisdom. The Lord created us to live under His benevolent authority. Then He instructed us to submit to the legitimate God-ordained human authorities in our lives as well. That was His plan for a life of supreme joy for those whom He made in His own image. But mankind fell under the spell of the original rebel: Satan. And sadly, many Christians have succumbed to this subtle deception of the enemy.

The American way is to stand up for your rights! Yet our Lord Jesus did not spend His life asserting His rights. He surrendered them in order to give that life to redeem us from the control of a malevolent foe. All authority was given to Jesus by the Father (Matthew 28:18). But He used that authority to always do those things that pleased His Father (John 8:29). In Hebrews 5:7 we're told that Jesus' prayers were heard "...because of his reverent submission." Christ described Himself as "gentle and humble in heart" (Matthew 11:29). That's a submissive spirit. That's humility. And He's our example in all things!

True human authority is exercised by one who is in submission. The centurion who sought healing from Jesus for his sick servant understood this principle. "Lord, I do not deserve to have you come under my roof. But just say the word, and my servant will be healed. For I myself am a man under authority, with soldiers under me. I tell this one, 'Go,' and he goes; and that one, 'Come,' and he comes. I say to my servant, 'Do this,' and he does it" (Matthew 8:8,9). Christ responded to the centurion's appeal by healing his servant. Biblical submission is a key to great blessing.

Many might be inclined to scorn a gentle spirit... maybe even to exploit it and become abusive. That's not God's way. He honors those who honor Him (I Samuel 2:30). And although my goodness cannot compare with the Lord's, I experienced a similar reaction to Tippy's wonderfully compliant attitude toward my wife and me. I was never tempted to take advantage of her. Her disposition drew greater love from me. I cherished her for her reverence of me.

9

Scripture clearly and repeatedly demonstrates how differently God feels toward the rebellious versus the submissive... the proud versus the humble. Psalm 138:6 informs us that "Though the Lord is on high, he looks upon the lowly, but the proud he knows from afar." James 4:6 reminds us that "God opposes the proud but gives grace to the humble."

In Psalm 119:21 we learn that the arrogant will receive God's rebuke, and if they don't repent, will suffer the curse that is the ultimate consequence of sin. Our Heavenly Father loves us too much to allow us to rush recklessly down the rebel road to destruction without a stern warning. He may even create situations to help turn our attitudes around. In Deuteronomy chapter 8, Moses revealed to God's people that their 40 years of wilderness wanderings were intended to do just that: "...to humble and to test you so that in the end it might go well with you" (verse 16).

You see, God's authority is not like that of a tyrant. Just like a proper earthly government's laws, His rules are intended for the good of individuals and society. The same Apostle John who proclaims that God is love (I John 4:16), instructs us that in return we must show our love to Him by obeying Him. And that obedience is not intended to be grievous. "This is love for God: to obey His commands. And His commands are not burdensome" (I John 5:3). Through submission to His will and His ways we're meant to discover the true pleasure of living.

It's wise to submit to the Lord. The reward of those submissive to Him is not only His watchful eye and His unearned favor, but His *esteem*. Hear the magnificent truth found in Isaiah 66:2: "This is the one I esteem: he who is humble... and trembles at my word." Imagine that! A lowly created human being enjoying high regard from the Almighty Creator. That's the prize for those who humbly submit to the Lord.

This world may be inclined to exploit the meek, but God loves and honors them. They even find places of leadership among His people. I doubt Moses could ever have won a primary race for the American presidency, let alone the general election. He wasn't assertive enough. You'd never find him publicizing how great he was. The Bible declares that "…Moses was a very humble man, more humble than anyone else on the face of the earth" (Numbers 12:3). Yet in the Lord's eyes he was one of the greatest leaders who ever lived.

I don't know about you, but I want to be much like Tippy in my Master's eyes. I want to have a submissive, obedient spirit. I want godly wisdom to prevail in my soul. I want my attitude to be a thing of beauty in His eyes. I want to be pleasing and useful to God. And I want to be blessed with His watchful care, His amazing grace, and His precious Presence.

Thank you, Father, for the illustrated sermon You gave me through my wise and beautiful canine companion: Tippy.

Chapter 4:
Re-Learning to Trust

Psalm 27:10 - "Though my father and mother
forsake me, the Lord will receive me."

LIKE MANY BABY BOOMERS, I grew up watching Lassie on the old black and white box. Under her charming influence, I fell in love with Collies. I never had a dog of my own as a child. It was a longing unfulfilled. So shortly after Carol and I got married, with her agreement, we began looking.

When we came across an ad for a Miniature Collie (officially known as a Shetland Sheep Dog, or Sheltie for short) free to a good home, I thought "close enough!" Shelties look like full sized Collies... *shrunk to apartment sized dimensions.* This one in particular had all the right markings to be a mini stand-in for Lassie. He was gorgeous.

His name was "Peanut." We weren't particularly fond of that handle. But as with most of our adopted dogs, who were also previously named, we didn't want to bring any more confusion and turmoil into a life that was already being severely disrupted by being torn from their former home.

Peanut took to Carol quickly. But he was reticent to bond with me. When I arrived home he would serenade me with a low rumbling growl from the top of the stairs that led to our apartment. It was a disappointment for a man who had been cheerfully anticipating an affectionate relationship with my first pet. We began to suspect that his problem with me was based on a bad experience with another man, likely his previous male owner. I was determined to win Peanut's trust. It took some time... but ultimately love triumphed.

Throughout my life I've come across many human souls wounded and sometimes even deformed by rejection. I believe trust is inherent in the newborn. It's only diminished (and sometimes eventually lost) through betrayal. Now, rejection in any close relationship can injure deeply. But the most powerful betrayal in a young life is unquestionably that of a mother or father. If a child loses the essential love of *both* mother *and* father the consequences are profound. The tragic result is often a bitter, lonely person, unable to build healthy relationships with anyone else.

Such tragedies deepen my appreciation for growing up in a loving Christian home. My parents set the stage for a lifetime of trusting the Lord. By example and precept they established a foundation of righteousness. Discipline, both corporal and otherwise, led me back to godly standards when I wandered. And *always*, the over-riding characteristic of our home was love... expressed in practical ways and through verbal and physical affection.

The lack of a *natural* point of reference from which to begin our understanding of a *supernatural* being's love is a huge obstacle for many in their search for God. It's hard to conceive of a loving *Heavenly* Father when your *earthly* dad was anything but.

Abusive parents tend to create an image of a God Who's constantly angry and disapproving. You're always awaiting the next painful slap. Cold, distant dads seem to reflect an aloof Creator, uninvolved in our day to day existence. Mothers and fathers who generate an emotional garbage can overflowing with unfulfilled promises, leave us struggling to have faith in God. And most devastating is when one or both parents abandon their children. We often end up assuming the Lord has abandoned us, too.

The first step in overcoming such spiritual and emotional handicaps is to recognize they exist. With the mind's capacity to bury painful memories and deny humiliating histories, that's not always as easy as it would seem. Often we mask insecurity with bluster and an outward display of false confidence.

That's why we're so dependent on the Lord's help to acknowledge our deepest needs. In Jeremiah 17:9,10 God shines the light of His truth on the problem. "The heart is deceitful above all things and beyond cure. Who can understand it? I the Lord search the heart and examine the mind..." If we allow Him, God will put His finger on the source of our trouble.

Once we come to realize how our personality has been distorted and our perspective of God warped by rejection, the door to His love is cracked open. If we're receptive enough to it, the revelation of that love may even arrive in one phenomenal moment... like a rushing torrent. More likely though, it'll be a process, as we gradually warm to His embrace and learn to trust Him.

The Lord may use another human being to demonstrate the reality of His love to us. After all, most Christians were led to the Savior by the influence of another person: a family member, friend, neighbor, co-worker, or preacher. God often chooses to use people to bring His glorious truths home to us.

Maybe Jesus wants to use you to demonstrate His love and faithfulness to someone who's lost faith. Or perhaps you're that wounded one spiritually growling at the approach of a loving God who only wants to adopt you as His own. Give Jesus a chance. You can learn to love and trust again!

Chapter 5:
Blind Love and Trust

I Peter 1:8 - "Though you have not seen him, you love him; and even though you do not see him now, you believe in him..."

DURING THE LAST COUPLE of years of his life, Tigger, one of our dearly loved Italian Greyhounds, gradually lost his sight. He had developed cataracts. They robbed him of his vision, but they couldn't steal his precious relationship with his masters. My wife, Carol, often referred to Tigger as her "lovey-dovey boy." He would stand (not sit!) on our laps, put his paws on either side of our necks, then affectionately tuck his head under our chins. It was adorable!

Tigger was a high energy guy. Early on, my son gave him the nickname "Spaz," short for "Spastic." Except for when he slept, or during those brief magic moments when he assumed the aforementioned hugging position, he rarely stood still. Tigger's frenetic movements were curtailed in those latter years, not so much by age, but by his visual disability. Yet he never lost his unique personality.

Blind though he was, Tigger's desire for the ones he could no longer see was unaffected. For the most part he depended on other senses to determine where we were, and seek us out. In spite of the cataracts that blurred our features beyond recognition, somehow he still managed to look me in the face. His diminished capacities may have hampered his movements, but his love and trust toward his masters remained rock solid.

Over the years I've thought about what it must have been like for the original followers of Jesus to physically see, hear, and touch Him.

How much greater would be the impact on my walk with God had I personally witnessed the compelling authority of His teaching, His overflowing compassion for the hurting and needy, His astounding miracles, and the pivotal moment in history when He rose from the dead? Would my measure of faith be greater? Would my zeal for advancing the Kingdom of God rise to an unimaginable level? I can only speculate.

Now the New Testament gives us an extensive account of one man who apparently *never saw* Jesus during the thirty-three years the Master's feet walked the earth. Yet we need not speculate about his later zeal for the One who eventually transformed his life. It was virtually boundless! I speak, as you have probably guessed, of Saul of Tarsus... a man who would ultimately be considered by most to be the greatest missionary of all time!

We first meet Saul in the opening verse of Acts chapter 8, where in retrospect of the previous chapter's account of the martyrdom of Stephen, Saul is noted as having been present at, and giving his approval to, that terrible deed. Acts chapter 9 begins by observing his continuing cruel campaign against those "...who belonged to the Way" (verse 2), this time in the city of Damascus. But Saul would soon undergo a career change, and a name change.

Before he could reach his destination, "...suddenly a light from heaven flashed around him." He heard the voice of the one he could not see. The man who had been the top persecutor of the church was about to become it's top promoter. After getting up from the ground and opening his eyes, the newly ordained Apostle realized he was blind. He had not seen Jesus of Nazareth. Now he couldn't see anything else either. But Saul had been the recipient of a new found love and faith. Three days later his physical sight would be supernaturally restored.

By Acts chapter 13, Saul of Tarsus had become Paul the Apostle. And the man who had never looked into the eyes of Jesus had become a devoted love slave of the One whose followers he had so viciously persecuted. Paul would traverse the Roman Empire, bringing countless thousands of Jews and Gentiles to faith in the Messiah, performing and receiving incredible miracles along the way.

And two-thousand years later, we are the beneficiaries of the thirteen New Testament books which flowed from his anointed pen.

All of us who've placed our trust in the Lord possess handicaps... even spiritual ones. Do we use them as excuses for not pursuing God as intensely as we ought? Do we allow these hindrances to ration our love for Him? Or do we with God's help find the strength to reach past our limitations to experience the unbounded joy of His Presence, and to fulfill the calling He's placed on each of our lives?

As long as we permit our limitations to dictate the level of our relationship with the Lord, our spiritual growth will be stunted. We'll be robbed of so much of the inheritance that's rightfully ours in Christ. Yes, we may sometimes grope about in darkness, every now and then even stumbling and falling. But we can trust the One Who understands our seasons of blindness. We can open our hearts to His divine love and love Him back... sight unseen!

In I Peter chapter 1, the apostle who once denied the Savior he could both see and touch, makes a powerful statement about his fellow believers. He asserts that they love and trust a Savior they've *never seen*. And this assertion occurs in the midst of a joyful expression of all the blessings that flow to us through Him Who is *invisible*. He ends his magnificat of praise for these unspeakable gifts by proclaiming that "Even angels long to *look into* these things" (verse 12).

Despite his declining senses, Tigger never surrendered his love and trust to the infirmities of age. He continued to grasp the benefits that were his through those who loved him and cared for his needs. And he never stopped reveling in what we meant to him.

Can we as God's dependents do less? Will we give in to the night of despair? Or will we hold fast our faith and love? I know the option I choose to pursue... how about you?

Chapter 6:
Secure in His Arms

Deuteronomy 33:27: - "...and underneath are the everlasting arms."

MORE THAN ONE VISITOR has marveled at the sight of a petite Italian Greyhound named Ranger cradled in my arms like an infant. Many dogs don't like to be held, and those who do, don't want it to be "belly up." You see, in canine protocol "belly up" means you're submitting to a superior power. It's a vulnerable position, and it's an acknowledgement that you're *not* the top dog. Now I've seen Ranger on occasion assert himself around other animals, even dogs many times his size. But he's never challenged *my* authority.

Ranger has always been comfortable in that exposed posture... *as long as he's in my arms.* For a dog who's been timid and fearful in other ways, it's remarkable. He trusts me implicitly in that regard. In fact, whenever he's in a situation which generates insecurity, he wants me to cradle him. He'll put his front paws on my leg, look me in the eye, and jump up and down until I pick him up. I'm never put off by this behavior. I actually find it engaging.

Where do you go when your senses are besieged by feelings of insecurity... when your "flight" instincts take over? We all have our escape mechanisms. Some of us indulge ourselves with comfort foods. Many turn to favorite movies or TV shows. Music may become the balm that soothes the troubled mind. A satisfying hobby becomes a pleasant distraction. Perhaps you phone a trusted friend or confidant. Maybe you go shopping. Unfortunately, some resort to less benign activities: things like drugs, alcohol, and illicit sex. In these they find the temporary comfort of an illusive dream world.

The first half of the Scripture verse which opens this chapter begins with an invitation from our Heavenly Father to let *Him* be our refuge. He wants us to trust that His everlasting arms will hold us up. That's not a God Who's annoyed when we put our paws on Him and beg to be held. Just as I'm more than willing to have Ranger surrender to the strength of my embrace, the Lord welcomes us to the refuge of His unequaled love and power.

This picture is not confined to a single verse in Scripture. The Word of God overflows with these kinds of divine metaphors. The Psalms in particular are replete with them. The Lord is described as our refuge, our rock, our fortress, our shelter, our shield, our strong tower... and the list could go on. All of us as believers can benefit from these powerful roles God wants to play in our lives.

Trouble is, many of us find it uncomfortable to acknowledge the frailties that should drive us into His arms. Men are conditioned to display nothing but confidence, never admitting weakness. Women are urged to be self-sufficient. Nowadays, even children are often encouraged to be independent of their parents, to be fearless and stand up for their rights. In such an environment, many find the image of being cradled like an infant an unwelcome one.

Yet our displays of unwavering self-confidence are often a front, masking deep insecurities we'd never reveal to others... even God. I've known a lot of self-confident people in my time. But I've never met one who didn't have moments of self-doubt, even if they wouldn't consciously acknowledge it to themselves, let alone others.

Of course, we should become less apprehensive as we mature in our faith. But we'll never reach the stage on this side of eternity where we don't periodically need to retreat into His shelter. All our bluster does is rob us of the comforting security to be discovered in the arms of the Almighty.

Now, what of those who do seek His support, but don't sense those loving arms beneath them? I think we all treasure those glorious mile-markers in life when God's Presence is so palpable that we get that tingling feeling all over. We wish we could live forever in the accompanying emotional high. But let's face it. God is sovereign and He doesn't always choose to do it that way.

Sometimes we can't detect any sign of His care. That's where a true and maturing trust in the Lord comes into play. II Corinthians 5:7 reminds us that "We live by faith, not by sight." …or sound … or touch… or emotion for that matter.

No one likes to "feel" the Holy Spirit more than I do. That exhilaration is one of the great joys of my life. Sometimes such an emotional reaction accompanies His benevolent intervention. But other times we don't feel a thing and simply have to take Him at His Word. Either way we can and should draw strength from His promise that "underneath are the everlasting arms."

Go ahead. Learn a lesson from a little dog called Ranger. Your Master may seem to be towering high above you, but He's just waiting for you to signal your desire to find refuge in His arms. Reach out to touch Him. Look into His tender eyes. And do a little jumping.

Chapter 7:
Love Is Forever

Jeremiah 3:14 - "'Turn, O backsliding children, saith the LORD; for I am married unto you...'" (KJV)

It was among the most difficult things I ever did. As a consequence, this is the most difficult chapter for me to write. It's a painful story to recount. But it illustrates too much valuable truth about the nature of God to remain untold.

Polo was the first dog we ever adopted as a *puppy*, the first one I ever house trained. He was a Dalmatian/Terrier mix, named after my young son's imaginary canine buddy. Like all of our dogs, he became a member of the family, and as such was deeply loved. Our youngest children, Matthew and Nicole, spent their early years growing up with this special hound. He was well-behaved for the first several years, until...

For some reason Polo turned destructive. He began tearing up the space where we left him when we went out. He started lifting his leg on our furniture. I was puzzled by this behavior. I couldn't put my finger on anything that might have triggered this change. We sought the advice of those locally whom we considered experts: veterinarians, trainers, etc. But no matter what I tried, Polo's detrimental activities continued. He was destroying my house. Having exhausted my limited resources for understanding and changing bad dog behavior, I'd reached the place where drastic measures became an unhappy imperative.

Let me make it clear that at this point in the story the typology which identifies me with the Lord breaks down somewhat. God's understanding of human nature is not limited as was my knowledge of canine nature. If I had known more about dogs back then, perhaps this tale would have a different ending. Nonetheless, the Bible tells us that there are times when in spite of His infinite wisdom, the Lord, too, must take drastic measures with wayward believers. We are after all, free-moral agents, able to defy His authority if we choose.

I reluctantly decided I would have to remove Polo from my house. I settled on a day and time when the kids would not be around to witness the departure of our beloved pet. I took Polo to our local SPCA to put him up for adoption, hoping that a change of environment would bring about a change in behavior. I embarrassed myself at the pound. As my heart ached, the tears began to flow and I found it a challenge to speak. Thankfully, the staff were understanding.

When the children arrived home and couldn't find Polo, I sat them down and explained as best I could. Every few days we called the SPCA to find out if he'd been adopted. We couldn't bear the thought of Polo being euthanized. In a week or so we were relieved to be told that he'd found a new home.

This experience illustrates two important truths about how God deals with His children. Number one: sometimes our bad decisions require severe discipline on the part of our Heavenly Father. Allow me here to make an important distinction between "discipline" and "retribution." Retribution is an end in itself. It's fair punishment for evil deeds. Discipline, on the other hand, is not an end in itself. Discipline maintains a view toward correction and restoration.

There are numerous examples of divine discipline in Scripture, but the one that best illustrates it in this context is provided in the letters to the church at Corinth. In I Corinthians chapter 5, the Apostle Paul dealt with a member of the church who was creating a sinful stench in the house of God. A brother was having immoral sexual relations with a woman who was apparently his stepmother. And the worst part is that he refused to stop! He wouldn't repent!

Paul rebuked the church for not dealing with the man's sin. He commanded them to expel the impenitent from the church, and have nothing to do with him. Paul even instructed his fellow believers to turn him over to the devil, "...so that the sinful nature may be destroyed and his spirit saved on the day of the Lord" (I Corinthians 5:5).

Sometimes sin has to run its destructive course before our stubborn wills yield to the truth. A prime example of this is the well-known parable of the prodigal son. In that much-loved story a wise and loving father releases his wayward son to pursue his devil-inspired lifestyle for a time.

Mercifully, the stern church discipline administered at Corinth was not the end of the story there, anymore than was the prodigal son's disastrous trip to a far country in Luke chapter 15. The son's slow descent into the pig pen brought him to his senses and ultimately back home. The strong medicine prescribed by Paul for the incestuous church member also produced its intended result. The backslider repented.

That brings us to truth <u>number two</u>: the Lord never stops loving His children. In II Corinthians 2:7,8, following the offender's repentance, the apostle directed the church members toward restoration. "Now instead, you ought to forgive and comfort him, so that he will not be overwhelmed by excessive sorrow. I urge you, therefore, to reaffirm your love for him."

That's the Bible pattern for God's dealings with rebels in the church. He loves them, but He won't allow them to destroy His house. I've rarely seen this kind of church discipline in my lifetime. Could it be that we've neglected a vital part of God's plan for managing destructive behavior in the Body of Christ?

But back to the case of Polo one more time. Because of his persistent harmful actions I had to expel him from my *house*... but he was never out of my *heart*. To this day I think of him with great fondness, and hope that his new life was a happy one. As appalling as his behavior was, my love for Polo never waned. That, I believe, is a picture of the Lord's undying love for us.

Our opening text teaches that the boundaries of God's relationship with us are astounding. In spite of our unfaithfulness… regardless of the dishonor our actions and attitudes bring to His Holy Name… His covenant remains intact! His commitment to His bride is unrelenting. The Lord says He is married to the backslider. If ever our love relationship with Him is to be broken, it will be *our* decision, not *His!*

Chapter 8:
Training

Hebrews 12:11 - "No discipline seems pleasant at the time,
but painful. Later on, however, it produces a harvest of
righteousness and peace for those who have been trained by it."

MOST OF OUR DOGS were adopted as adults, and came to us already house-trained. But two of them entered our home as recently weaned puppies: Polo and Tippy. It was my responsibility to train them. I taught them a few important basic commands such as "Sit, Stay, and Come." The chief part of their education, however, was learning to do their "business" outside.

Thankfully, both Polo and Tippy were relatively easy to train. But it was interesting to watch their initial reaction to the process. Neither understood why they were being taken outdoors for lengthy periods, and not allowed to re-enter the house until they'd done their business. Why did the master insist on this practice, and why did he seem so happy when they pottied outside?

In particular, I remember taking Tippy into the backyard one night during this training period. We'd been out for quite a while, waiting for her to do her thing. She hadn't fully caught on yet, and appeared puzzled and a bit frustrated about this marathon. I guess she simply wanted to go back into the house and relax. Many years later I can still see that adorable little puppy face of hers in the light of the porch lamp. She finally laid down, then rested her head on my foot and looked up at me as if to say: "What's this all about? Can't we just go back inside, Daddy?"

Whether they understand it or not, all pets need this discipline. Life involves a great deal of routine, and the right kind of routine is established by good habits. The routines that result from proper dog training pave the way for a happy future. They bring pleasure to the master and his household and establish a satisfying and healthy lifestyle for the family dog. But our pooches don't necessarily connect these benefits to their training course. They just *endure* the training… then *enjoy* the benefits.

Often God's kids also fail to grasp the value of discipline. Like little Tippy we gaze into our Heavenly Father's eyes with a look that pleads "Why?" Maybe we need to remember that the Master has called us to be His *disciples*, and the root word for that calling is *discipline*. Like it or not, discipline and training are essential elements of the true Christian life.

Look again at the Bible verse that begins this discussion on training. The Lord reminds us that despite the unpleasantness and pain that often accompany discipline, its outcome is good. It yields righteousness and peace to its practitioners. In fact, in Hebrews 12:8 the case is made that a lack of godly training is an indication we may not be true sons and daughters of God!

Training works best when it begins early. The old adage "You can't teach an old dog new tricks" may not be entirely true, but it surely points toward reality. Yes, you *can* get to Florida through Alaska, but the trip will go a lot better if you start out headed in the right direction. You'll arrive with more energy in reserve and with a lot less frustration.

That's why the Lord instructed His people to "Train a *child* in the way he should go, and when he is old he will not turn from it" (Proverbs 22:6). And what works in the natural usually has a parallel in the spiritual. That's why it's so vital that new believers are directed toward the proper onramp at the start of their journey.

Understand, Redemption Road is not simply a freeway to Heaven, it's a training course as well. Those who maneuver it best understand that though the destination is critical, the trip is important, too. Otherwise God may as well take us directly to Heaven the moment we're saved. Get it?

The analogy of God as our Father and life as a journey to our home in Heaven is one that helps us understand how important spiritual training is. There are, however, other metaphors. Scripture compares us not only to travelers, but to warriors (Psalm 144:1), students (Luke 6:40), and athletes (I Corinthians 9:25). In each case the discipline of rigorous training is indispensable, and that training is both for our good and God's glory.

Now, the Lord works personally with each of us to teach us how to live, and help us develop godly habits. He's given us all access to His Word, and His Spirit dwells in every born again Christian. Those are the key elements of our spiritual training. We need to allow God to work through them. It's imperative that we study the Bible regularly and learn to be sensitive to the Holy Spirit's promptings. The Lord will use these channels to get us, and keep us, on course.

But He also uses His mature servants to help train us. The Great Commission was not limited to getting people saved and then leaving it at that. Jesus commanded His followers to "...go and *make disciples* of all nations..." (Matthew 28:18). Experienced believers have a God-ordained hand in teaching new believers how to live.

The first place that discipline begins is in our families. The law of God didn't charge the priests with training children in the commandments of the Lord. That responsibility belonged to parents. "Teach them to your children, talking about them when you sit at home and when you walk along the road, when you lie down and when you get up" (Deuteronomy 11:19).

From there God may also assign other spiritual mentors throughout our journey to assist in guiding us in godly principles and habits. Pastors, teachers, and other seasoned servants of the Lord fill that bill nicely.

Do you want to please God? "So we make it our goal to please him..." (II Corinthians 5:9). Do you want to live a fulfilling life? "For physical training is of some value, but godliness has value for all things, holding promise for both the present life and the life to come" (I Timothy 4:8). Godly training does exact a price, but the spiritual dividends are exponential!

Chapter 9:
The Power of Perseverance

Luke 18:5 - "…yet because this widow keeps bothering me, I will see that she gets justice, so that she won't eventually wear me out with her coming!"

It's common knowledge among breeders that Italian Greyhounds can be stubborn. Ranger might very well be the poster boy (or should that be poster dog?) for that generally unappreciated canine trait. But there's an upside to stubbornness. Aimed in the right direction it can become a positive force known as "perseverance." Let me paint a couple of typical scenarios for you from the life and times of my little buddy Ranger.

It's mealtime. And since Ranger is self-feeding (pooch talk for eat whenever you want), that could be just about any hour of the day. One of his personal favorites is what we like to call his late night snackypoo (is that actually a word?). That usually happens sometime around 9:00 or 10:00 PM when my wife and I go to bed. But whenever mealtime happens to be, the relentless side of Ranger's nature takes over when he discovers his bowl is empty.

Carol and I haven't yet noticed that he's out of food. No problem for Ranger. First he begins scratching the bowl. If we don't observe it the first time, he scratches again… louder. Maybe we're preoccupied. If the continued scratching doesn't work, the barking starts. That could go on for a while. We could be in another part of the house. Which leads to the final step. Ranger seeks us out and begins his whining and crying routine. For canine loving softies like my wife and me, that pathetic appeal will do the trick. Ranger's bowl is now filled.

Here's another mental image for you: Ranger is on my lap. I'm petting him, rubbing his neck, or otherwise giving him some kind of physical affection. He's eating it up. After a while I stop. Ranger uses his multi-purpose nose to nudge my hand back into position. Once more I respond to his craving for a loving caress. When I tire or my attention wanders, again that pointy little snout appeals for more emotional warmth from his master's touch and I'm back at it. Yes, canine persistence pays.

There's an obvious spiritual metaphor here. For His own reasons God has ordained that perseverance should be a significant part of our walk with Him. He could answer our prayers and bring His Word to fruition in an instant... and sometimes He does. But it appears in both Scripture and personal experience that the Lord usually first requires perseverance on our part.

"Perseverance" and its corollary "patience" occur nearly thirty times in the New Testament, not to mention other synonyms like "endurance," "persistence," and "diligence." The concept is so woven into the fabric of the Christian life that to try to remove it would result in the unraveling of the whole garment.

As with all Christian virtues, Jesus is our best example of godly persistence. In urging the believers in Thessalonica to continue in the faith, Paul expresses this desire: "May the Lord direct your hearts into God's love and Christ's perseverance" (II Thessalonians 3:5). And since God is love, and perseverance is a fruit of love (I Corinthians 13:7), it's no surprise that the loving Son of God should demonstrate perseverance in its highest form. He endured unimaginable suffering in order to obtain the prize of our redemption.

For the *followers* of Christ, perseverance also holds the assurance of a reward. The inspired author of the book of Hebrews understood this. In Hebrews 10:36 he urged his readers: "You need to persevere so that when you have done the will of God, you will receive what he has promised." Further, he recommends the example of the Old Testament saints: "We do not want you to become lazy, but to imitate those who through faith and patience inherit what has been promised" (Hebrews 6:12).

Want to receive something from the Lord that He's promised in the Bible? Jesus counseled us to persevere. "Ask and it will be given to you; seek and you will find; knock and the door will be opened to you" (Matthew 7:7). To fully grasp this formula you need to be aware that the tense of the words *ask*, *seek*, and *knock* in the original Greek is the perfect present tense. In other words Jesus was instructing us to *keep on asking, keep on seeking, and keep on knocking.*

In Luke chapter 18 the Savior presented a parable of persistence to encourage us to press through in prayer. It told of a judge without a conscience and a widow without an off switch. She repeatedly sought justice from this unfit man of the bench. For a while he refused her requests. He didn't care about anyone but himself. It was that self-concern, coupled with her non-stop motor, that ultimately brought justice to the plaintiff. Hear again the judge's own words revealed at the top of this chapter: "...yet because this widow keeps bothering me, I will see that she gets justice, so that she won't eventually wear me out with her coming!"

At the end of the story Jesus declared: "Listen to what the unjust judge says. And will not God bring about justice for his chosen ones, who cry out to him day and night? Will he keep putting them off? I tell you, he will see that they get justice, and quickly" (verses 6-8).

Are you like Ranger gazing at an empty dish? Let your Master know about it. Remember, Jesus didn't teach us to ask once and then forget about it. He taught us to pray *daily* for our bread (Matthew 6:11). Like Ranger are you craving an expression of love from your Master? Nudge Him repeatedly by spending time in the Word and prayer. In that Blessed Book Christ reminds His disciples: "As the Father has loved me, so have I loved you. Now remain in my love" (John 15:9).

Let me close this chapter by reminding you of the whole reason why Jesus shared the parable of the unjust judge I mentioned above. In Luke 18:1 that account is prefaced with these words: "Then Jesus told his disciples a parable to show them that they should always pray and not give up."

Chapter 10:
The Nature of Competition

Romans 12:10 - "Honor one another above yourselves."

FOR MORE THAN A dozen years, stable mates Tigger and Ranger shared our home and our love. As canine relationships go, their's was a pretty good one. They never really fought, bit, or injured one another. On occasion they played together. Sometimes they'd cuddle. There were even moments when one would look out for the other. Like when Ranger noticed that Tigger was wanting to get back into the house. He'd notify us by barking and leading us to the door where Tigger was waiting.

Times of cooperation aside, they remained competitors. Tigger's role as alpha dog seemed to make it tough for him to engage much in games with Ranger. And when he did, he'd often *dominate* rather than *play*. Sometimes he found it necessary to assert himself by making Ranger move from a spot in which Ranger had just made himself comfortable. Then he'd take over that cozy warmed and prepared site rather than find one of his own.

Although they never actually fought over food, they would once in a while engage in a bit of rivalry over some delectable morsels, even to the point of growling and baring teeth. Tigger usually won those challenges. But in later years, as Tigger grew blind, Ranger would take advantage and steal Tigger's treats as he lost track of them. Another example of their rivalry was that if one noticed the other receiving attention and affection, he invariably grew jealous and tried to horn in on the attention. When competition reigns, jealousy frequently sours otherwise healthy relationships.

Those doggy mini-dramas played out in front of us usually illustrated the *downside* of this thing we call competition. On the upside, playful competition can be fun and relaxing. And godly competition, which contends simply for the prize (I Corinthians 9:24), not to outdo someone else, can result in great achievements that honor God and benefit mankind. Unfortunately, most of the time competition is selfish and destructive, particularly in terms of interpersonal relationships.

That's why you don't see competition among Christians encouraged in the Word of God. Indeed, the teachings of Scripture commonly *discourage* it. In the race to be foremost in the Kingdom of God, Jesus taught that the first will be last and the last will be first (Mark 9:35). And He asserted that the greatest among us must be the servant of all. That's the reverse of how the world system views it!

Achievements do have value in God's eyes. But they must be accomplished according to God's methods. Any effort which leaves wounded and broken relationships in its wake cannot enjoy divine blessing. The Bible puts a greater premium on relationships than on achievements. That's why Christ decreed " Love the Lord your God with all your heart and with all your soul and with all your mind. This is the first and greatest commandment. And the second is like it: Love your neighbor as yourself" (Matthew 22:37-39).

The core values of the predominate culture are revealed in philosophies that tout the preeminence of "self-love" and "self-esteem." While some level of those principles may be needed in life, God never puts them anywhere near the top of *His* list. "Always look out for number one" is not a phrase you'll find anywhere in Scripture. Instead, we're instructed to make our love relationship with God top priority. Second to that is our relationship with our fellow man. Then where does our perceived need to view others as competitors, rather than brothers and sisters to be loved unselfishly, fit into that equation?

It doesn't! Nonetheless, worldly competition has often been woven as a prevailing pattern into the fabric of the church. In my decades of involvement in Christian ministry I've observed it far too much. It wounds rather than heals. It's a terrible witness to outside observers. And it grieves the heart of God.

Sometimes the predominance of ungodly competition is obvious. It reaches an ugly zenith that results in the winner glorying in the humiliation of the loser. Other times it's deviously subtle.

I remember many years ago how a fellow pastor and friend shared excitedly about how God had moved his small congregation to give a sacrificially large amount of money in a special offering. My response? ...one-ups-man-ship! I bragged about how our people had collected an even larger amount of money. Ostensibly I was commending our church and glorifying the Lord. But my motives were not that pure. It wasn't until *after* I uttered those words that I realized what I had done.

God wants us not to step on one another as we race toward the goal. He urges us to "Carry each other's burdens, and in this way you will fulfill the law of Christ" (Galatians 6:2). Romans chapter 12 abounds with some wonderfully pithy truths along these lines. One is found at the beginning of this discussion on the nature of competition. Here are just a few others in that impressive list: "Love must be sincere. Be devoted to one another in brotherly love. Live in harmony with one another. Bless those who persecute you... Do not be conceited. Do not repay anyone evil for evil. Do not take revenge..."

As their caring masters, Carol and I always drew pleasure from those moments when the relationship between Tigger and Ranger was symbiotic - not adversarial. And I have no doubt that our Heavenly Father feels the same about the interaction among His children.

Lord, please make us more sensitive to our motivations. Help us to love our neighbors more. And transform us increasingly into the likeness of our selfless older brother, Jesus.

Chapter 11:
The Joy of Your Presence

Psalm 16:11 - "...you will fill me with joy in your presence."

DOGS ARE SOCIAL CREATURES. That's the primary reason why more American homes have dogs as pets that any other animal. True, they can be valuable working animals. Many make their living on farms and ranches, or by the side of hunters. They may serve as guides for the blind. Some make fine watch or guard dogs. Thousands earn their keep as racers or entertainers. And that's an abridged list of useful bow-wow careers. Still, the chief role they fill for people is that of companionship.

It seems no other creature on the planet becomes so attached to humans. Once a loving relationship is established between canine and master, dogs can become like Velcro. And while that kind of attachment may be an annoyance to some, it's a winsome attribute to most dog owners.

My sentiments rest with the latter group. In fact, the older I get, the deeper my appreciation for my pet's desire to be around me. I've progressed from having medium sized dogs who recline *near* me, to owning lap dogs who rest *on* me.

Now let's face it. Our hounds don't always have pure motives for hanging around us. Sometimes they're just hoping for a remnant of our snack. Reality may force me to admit in those instances that they're only lingering to get something out of me. Nonetheless, even then I enjoy their company. Is that so bad?

In the Bible verse above, the Psalmist anticipates joy in the Presence of the Lord. We should, too. That joy may stem from a blessing we want from Him. It is, after all, inherent in the divine nature for God to give good things to His children (Matthew 7:11). But the highest reason for seeking the Lord's Presence is simply for the love of Him. That pleases His great heart the most.

Two of God's most honored leaders clearly valued His Presence above all. Following Israel's wilderness sin of creating an idol in the form of a golden calf, Moses' intercession averted God's judgment. Still, the Lord was going to withdraw His Presence from those stiff-necked people, and instead provide an angel to pave the way into the promised land. Once more Moses interceded. In Exodus 33:15 that righteous leader demonstrated his high regard for God's Presence when he said to the Lord: "If your presence does not go with us, do not send us up from here."

After his repentance for his sins of adultery and murder, King David did not express fear of losing his throne, his riches, or his prestige. Psalm 51:11 indicates where he felt his real fortune lay. "Do not cast me from your presence or take your Holy Spirit from me."

Moses and David loved God deeply, and did not want to go through life without His glorious Presence. So how do we enter and maintain this wonderful Presence of the Lord? It's important at this juncture to distinguish among three different forms of His Presence: omnipresence, covenant presence, and manifest presence.

Omnipresence is God's existence everywhere in the universe at the same time. But omnipresence is not conditional, and carries with it no promise of His favor or blessing. It simply means He's everywhere at once. It doesn't signify any type of relationship with people.

The Lord's *covenant presence* belongs exclusively to those who enter into covenant with Him. The Old Covenant, which was given to the Jews through His laws and commandments, was sealed by the blood of a sacrificial lamb. It anticipated a New Covenant yet to come. That New Covenant was sealed by the blood of the Lamb of God: Jesus. It now reconciles to a holy God all sinners who enter into it through repentance and faith. This is referred to as being "born again" (John 3:3). From that moment on we're promised God's unbroken covenant presence. In both the Old and New Testaments

He pledges never to leave us nor forsake us (Deuteronomy 31:6, Hebrews 13:5). But we're not always consciously aware of God's covenant presence.

On the other hand, the *manifest presence* of God is that which can be recognized by our senses or emotions. To a large degree, the manifest presence of God is dispensed as He sovereignly chooses, though we can encourage these manifestations by our godly attitudes and actions. God's covenant presence is taken by faith even when there's no sign of it. His manifest presence is demonstrable. It's the kind of encounter with the Lord that we yearn for in this life.

We enter into God's covenant presence through the born again experience mentioned earlier. But the Lord decides how and when to display His manifest presence. As I said, however, we may promote the manifest presence of God in our lives. Scripture indicates we can do this through acts of devotion such as Bible reading, prayer, praise, and worship.

Now, there is no human counterpart to omnipresence or covenant presence for us when it comes to our relationship with our pets. Those are strictly divine attributes. Our manifest presence, so to speak, is what they revel in. When we return home our dogs celebrate. They often perform the canine equivalents of singing and dancing. They love being with us. And we love it, too!

What do our dogs do when we're not around and they miss us? Like believers who long for the manifest presence of the Lord, our pets await with yearning their next encounter with us. But that's not all. The next best thing to having us there is finding something that is a powerful reminder of us: our scent. It may be on our bed, a favorite chair, or perhaps a pair of shoes. Until we return, they spend time with that object which provides a comforting connection of sorts.

Someday when Christ returns for His own, we'll be transported to our eternal home where His Presence is forever manifest to His people. Meanwhile, as we wait for the next earthly manifestation of His joyful Presence, we search out those things that carry His sweet scent. We spend time in the Word... we pray, praise, and worship...

we sing or listen to Christian music... we fellowship with others who bear His likeness... and we go to church.

So if you find yourself in one of those spiritually dry places, remember: in all those sacred things we find some measure of the joy we experience in His actual manifest presence. We're also encouraging the next divine visitation. Plus, know that in the process He draws pleasure from our pursuit of Him. So keep seeking the objects that release His divine fragrance. Perhaps we'll soon thrill to the next experience of God's manifest presence!

Chapter 12:
We Need the Fire

I Thessalonians 5:19 - "Do not put out the Spirit's fire..."

ITALIAN GREYHOUNDS (ALSO KNOWN as Iggies) are amazing diminutive athletes. They're built for speed and they can jump as if their hind legs were pogo sticks. But the selective breeding that emphasized those abilities, left them with virtually no body fat. Plus, they have only minimal short fur. So they lack the protection against cold temperatures enjoyed by other breeds.

For many years Carol and I were blessed with a pair of Iggy companions. Some of our dogs romped and played in the snow. Not these two. They despised winter weather. If humans hadn't already done so, I'm sure Tigger and Ranger would have been credited with the discovery of fire. Their favorite hangout when the mercury plunged, was in front of the wood stove or the fireplace. They staked out their turf so close to the flames that we were astounded they didn't disappear in a puff of smoke!

Tigger and Ranger loved the fire. They loved it because they needed it. It drove away the coldness and warmed their bodies. It covered their weakness... in this case a lack of natural insulation from nature's cold cruel temperatures.

And what of us, my friend? Do we love the fire? Do we recognize our frailties enough to seek it, then camp out as near to it as we can? Do we let its energy transform our shivering, shrinking spirits?

At this point, of course, I speak not of physical fire, but of the spiritual flames which come from God Himself. In Deuteronomy 4:24, and again in Hebrews 12:29, we're told that "God is a consuming fire." As with physical fire, His spiritual fire can burn or bless. It can judge sin and unrepentant sinners. Or it can radiate light and warmth for the righteous. How we experience the fire of God depends on us.

Even as born again believers we still have weaknesses that need the beneficial effects of the fire. God majors in exchanging His strength for our weakness. We see examples of it throughout the Bible. Truth be told, He chooses the weak in order to glorify His own power. I Corinthians 1:27 tells us so: "God chose the weak things of the world to shame the strong."

The Apostle Paul discovered this through what he terms "a thorn in my flesh." Scripture doesn't disclose exactly what this thorn in the flesh was, but Paul does admit it was a weakness of some sort. Three times he asked the Lord to deliver Him from it. God's response offers us insight into His nature. "My grace is sufficient for you, for my power is made perfect in weakness" (II Corinthians 12:9).

Paul didn't reject the Lord's counsel. He embraced it. Here's what Paul said in reaction: "Therefore I will boast all the more gladly about my weaknesses, so that Christ's power may rest on me. That is why, for Christ's sake, I delight in weaknesses, in insults, in hardships, in persecutions, in difficulties. For when I am weak, then I am strong" (II Corinthians 12:9,10).

God speaks through fire. In Deuteronomy 5:4 Moses reminded the Children of Israel that the Lord had used flames to communicate with them. "The Lord spoke to you face to face out of the fire on the mountain." We, too, need to see the Word of God exhibited powerfully, so that we recognize its majesty and authority. As we pointed out earlier, our God is a consuming fire!

The fire of God, which is a provision of His grace, is medicine for our infirmities in several ways. It purges our sinful guilt (Isaiah 6:6,7). It refines our character, bringing the impurities to the surface where they can be purged (Zechariah 13:9, I Peter 1:17). It sheds light on our path to give us direction (Exodus 13:21). It overcomes our fleshly resistance to doing the will of God (Jeremiah 20:9). And it empowers us as spokesmen for the Most High (Psalm 39:3).

The latter provision is what John the Baptist spoke of when in Matthew 3:10 he declared; "I baptize you with water for repentance. But after me will come one who is more powerful than I, whose sandals I am not fit to carry. He will baptize you with the Holy Spirit and with fire." In Acts 1:8 Christ made the purpose of this fire plain. "But you will receive power when the Holy Spirit comes on you; and you will be my witnesses in Jerusalem, and in all Judea and Samaria, and to the ends of the earth."

Everywhere we turn we discover how essential the Lord's flames are to His people. No wonder in this chapter's primary text we're commanded not to quench the Holy Spirit's fire. God's fire must be constantly burning. He assigned this awesome responsibility to His servants in Leviticus 6:13. "The fire must be kept burning on the altar continuously; it must not go out."

Are you encumbered by weakness? Feeling cold about the things of the Spirit? Then like Tigger and Ranger gather around the fire. Read and study the Word of God. Pray for the fire to fall in your life. Get out to church services where the flames of the Holy Spirit are at work.

Don't keep shivering in the winter of your spirit. Bask in the warmth and energy of the Lord's provision for that chill that's gripping your heart. Face reality. You need the fire, and so do I.

Chapter 13:
Let Me Do My Thing

*Proverbs 14:12 - "There is a way that seems right
to a man, but in the end it leads to death."*

THE FIRST TIME I attempted to attach a leash to Peanut's collar, I encountered a curious reaction. He twisted his head and neck in various directions, making it difficult for me make the connection. This handsome Shetland Sheep Dog wanted no part of restraint. I soon discovered the reason for his resistance. Peanut was a "car chaser."

He was an otherwise agreeable pet. We loved and enjoyed Peanut. But something about an internal combustion motor vehicle moving past him sparked his chase impulse. Now, running after a rabbit or squirrel can involve risk on occasion. But racing a two-ton or larger moving machine is clearly hazardous… at least that's how a dog's *master* sees it.

My effort to control Peanut was not an expression of my dictatorial thirst for control. It was designed to protect him. Leashing Peanut was an act of love. He didn't see it that way. He viewed that six foot strap as an unwarranted restriction that kept him from doing his thing.

There's a lesson for God's children in all of this. Human nature can be as averse to restraint as canine nature. Do you know anyone who inherently enjoys rules that obstruct what they consider personal pleasures? Me either.

In the Garden of Eden God blessed Adam and Eve with rich pleasures beyond anything we've ever experienced. They were the apex of a perfect creation. They lived in a paradise of unimaginable beauty. No sickness, no death, and no wars in this blissful home. They fellowshipped daily with a loving Heavenly Father. They feasted on foods more luscious than anything we've known since. Only *one* restriction. God said: "…you must not eat from the tree of the knowledge of good and evil, for when you eat of it you will surely die" (Genesis 2:17).

Satan approached them in the body of a serpent and planted a seed of discontent. "Did God really shackle your appetites?" The Devil began by appealing to their tummies. Then he appealed to their egos. "Go ahead and eat the forbidden fruit. You won't die. God lied. He just wants to spoil your fun. He knows when you eat that food you'll become gods like Him."

Our ancient ancestors fell for the lie. Eve looked again at the banned delicacy and found it alluring. Without the truth to hold her back anymore she took it and ate it. Adam followed suit. Death shrouded life, and mankind learned its first lesson the hard way.

Doing your own thing may be the way of this fallen world, but it's not the path to the good life the Lord intends for His own. Jesus made it clear who has our best interests at heart, and it's not Satan with the worldly values he promotes. In John 10:10 the Savior says: "The thief comes only to steal and kill and destroy; I have come that they may have life, and have it to the full."

The law of God points us in the right direction. But we inevitably fall short. The grace of God in Jesus Christ restores us, and we want to continue in that grace.

Those who respect divinely *imposed discipline* will ultimately develop the *self-control* that is the fruit of the Spirit (Galatians 5:22,23) who lives within every true believer. And they'll discover that those restraints the old nature interprets as *joy-killers* are ultimately *life-savers*.

As a child of God you have a choice to make every time the Master stoops down to connect you to His life-line. Like Peanut you can say "Let me do my thing!" You can twist, contort, and turn away from His influence. Or you can yield to the One who knows what's best for you.

Yes, that means acknowledging you don't know it all. And that's humbling in an ungodly system that puts a premium on being master of your own fate and doing your own thing. Still, the rewards of doing God's thing are far greater than any status you might gain among those who cast off divine rule, by surrendering to your own perilous cravings.

Numbers chapter 11 gives the account of people who became discontented with the Lord's provision. During their wilderness wanderings God had provided the Children of Israel with a miracle food they called "manna." They didn't have to farm or hunt for their food. It just appeared. They simply had to gather and prepare it. It supplied all the healthy nutrition they needed.

But it was too bland for some of them. They complained bitterly about this restrictive diet. Mouths drooling, they recited the menu from the years of their Egyptian bondage. "If only we had meat to eat!" they cried. "We were better off in Egypt!" (Numbers 11:18)

God gave them what they demanded. But the meat they yearned for brought them sickness and death. The site of the mass graves of those who fell was given a name that says it all. "Kibroth Hattaavah" literally means "graves of craving." That story is recounted in the Bible with the hope that we'll learn our lesson the easy way.

Pursuing that which is outside the Lord's wise provision can prove fatal. Now, premature physical death is something we want to prevent. But the second death of which the Scriptures speak is to be avoided at all costs! Eternal separation from God is a fate worse than the grave. And playing with sin is the onramp of the freeway to hell.

So when you're tempted to shirk the Lord's leash, remember He's not being a kill-joy. He's looking out for your best interests. He's keeping you on the path of life and away from the highway to death. Deny your carnal impulses in that critical moment... and thank God for His loving care!

Chapter 14:
Flee Fleas

I Corinthians 15:33 - "Do not be misled: Bad company corrupts good character."

THE LATE BAPTIST PREACHER and Christian comedian, Grady Nutt, once lamented that Noah could have saved the rest of us a lot of grief if he'd just left chiggers (those nasty little mites that feed on human skin) off the ark. Dogs might be inclined to also complain about the inclusion among the passengers of those blood-sucking critters called fleas. Flea bites leave them with a maddening itch that can lead to fur loss. Suffer enough of these parasites and our pets can even end up anemic!

Our beloved canine buddy Polo could have testified as to how unpleasant fleas can make one's existence. His unhappy experience began when some folks from our church kindly offered to take care of him while we vacationed for a week. As with all our dogs, Polo was a *house* pet. We didn't realize that our benefactors were planning to keep him in their *barn*.

Poor Polo... when we picked him up after vacation we were led to the temporary quarters he shared with all the barn-dwelling animals. We soon discovered that our pooch had contracted a massive infestation of fleas from his week long residency. He was miserable. It took a major prolonged effort to rid Polo of his tormentors. We made sure to arrange for more beneficial accommodations and companionship for him during our future family excursions.

As Christians, the places we hang out and the company we keep can be beneficial or detrimental. And sometimes it doesn't take very long for the effect to transpire. We need to be prudent. I remember a verse from a childhood Sunday School song. Three times it warned: "Be careful little feet where you go." Why? "For the Father up above is looking down in love."

I grew up in a church era of great emphasis on personal holiness. At times that emphasis was overwrought. It occasionally reached beyond the clear teachings of Scripture into an arena of manmade legalism. Some of the rules and standards promoted were downright silly.

Since then the pendulum has generally swung in the opposite direction… *too far*. We now live in an age of Christianity diluted by what some have termed "easy believeism," and "cheap grace." It sometimes seems that for the contemporary believer anything goes.

The Lord didn't intend holiness and sanctification to cramp our style. He established these principles to allow us to live lives that demonstrate Who He is to others, and to keep our days on earth spiritually healthy and satisfying. We need to rediscover the essential value of being careful where our feet take us.

Of course, in a world where our "physical feet" can easily become "virtual feet" by way of ubiquitous mass media, the phrase "where you go," from the aforementioned children's Sunday School song takes on new meaning. Television, radio, print media, and the internet can also take us to places where spiritual fleas can suck the life out of our relationship with God. We need to allow the Word of God and the Spirit of God to direct us in exercising discrimination in our journeys.

"Discrimination…" now there's a word that has fallen into disrepute. That descent began with the use of the word in connection with racism. And certainly racial discrimination is detestable. But in recent decades the politically correct idea that "discrimination" against all manner of ungodly lifestyles is wrong, has further transformed this perfectly legitimate term into a dirty word.

We need to realize that discrimination is only bad when it operates outside the parameters of Scripture. Indeed, the child of

God has an obligation to the Lord, himself, fellow believers, and the lost, to be discriminating.

Does that mean we should have no contact with sinful people? Certainly not! How can we possibly bear witness of a *loving* Savior to the lost without *loving* interaction? The key is making sure that the most powerful influences in our lives are godly ones. We need to take care that our closest relationships and our most contagious environments are holy ones.

When making those choices we might want to ponder the question posed long ago by one of history's most powerful evangelists. Billy Sunday asked: "If you throw a polecat (skunk) into a parlor, which will change first… the polecat (skunk) or the parlor?" Considering the dramatic potential consequences, we need to seek divine wisdom before we make these kinds of decisions.

In the Old Testament the Lord repeatedly admonished His people to take every precaution not to allow pagan values to infiltrate their individual and corporate lives. In II Corinthians 6:14 Paul makes the issue clear to New Testament saints as well. "Do not be yoked together with unbelievers. For what do righteousness and wickedness have in common? Or what fellowship can light have with darkness?"

Is there an unrelenting itch distracting you in your walk with God? Is the fur flying as your protective coat is deteriorating? Is your spiritual life becoming anemic? Ask the Master to deliver you from those ungodly parasites. Then follow the wisdom that is from above when it comes to where you go and who you spend your time with. Spiritually speaking, "Flee fleas!"

Chapter 15:
The Search

Proverbs 25:2 - "It is the glory of God to conceal a matter; to search out a matter is the glory of kings."

THERE'S A GAME MY wife, Carol, loves to play with our dogs. It usually begins right after we arrive home, or one or more of our canine buddies returns to the house from outdoors. Carol finds a place to hide. She may stand behind a door or crouch beside a piece of furniture. The dogs search passionately from room to room and place to place. Their pursuit may end in a quick success, or develop into a more lengthy challenge. In the latter case she or I will sometimes offer a hint.

The instinct for the hunt is innate in hounds. They were born for this. Their senses of sight, sound, and smell are heightened. Such enthusiasm in the search leads to an effervescent celebration at the moment of discovery!

It's hard to say who enjoys this process and its culmination more. Our pets revel in the pursuit, and dance with glee at the finish line. Carol and I also delight in the game. It evokes broad smiles and pleasant laughter. Ultimately we greet the victors with congratulatory affection.

It's not hard to see how dogs draw great pleasure from their search for such hidden treasure. But when *God's children* are the searchers and our *Heavenly Father* is the one doing the concealing, it's often difficult for us to find joy in the journey. More often than not we experience frustration, confusion, and discouragement.

Perhaps no one in Scripture expresses these typically human feelings more transparently than Job. He lost his children, his riches, and his health. His friends condemned him while his God fell silent. Feel his exasperation: "If only I knew where to find him; if only I could go to his dwelling! …But if I go to the east, he is not there; if I go to the west, I do not find him. When he is at work in the north, I do not see him; when he turns to the south, I catch no glimpse of him" (Job 23:3,8,9).

Like Job of old, we're sometimes bewildered by the maze of our lives. The blessings that once characterized our walk with the Lord have given way to inscrutable tribulations. Faith and trust are assailed by doubt and uncertainty. Where is the "pearl of great value" (Matthew 13:45,46) we thought we'd discovered? We bought into this so-called treasure and now it seems to have disappeared.

We forget that Jesus declared to those who would follow Him: "In this world you will have trouble. But take heart! I have overcome the world" (John 16:33). Like you, I'd prefer a spiritual experience akin to a pleasant walk through the garden or along the beach with a friend… everything of enthralling beauty in clear view. So frequently, however, our surroundings are troubling and mystifying. We weary of the quest for God's purposes and wonder where He's hiding and why.

We need to bear in mind that as our opening text asserts, the Lord's ways include occasions when He conceals His plans and purposes. Sometimes He even hides Himself. The prophet Isaiah recognizes this aspect of God's dealings with His people in chapter 45, verse 15: "truly you are a God who hides himself…" And II Chronicles 32:31 refers to a period in the life of godly King Hezekiah when: "…God left him to test him and know everything that was in his heart."

Be encouraged by recognizing that even Christ Himself suffered through disquieting thoughts in an intensely troubling time. Suspended between heaven and earth on a torturous cross in unimaginable anguish, His perplexed soul cried out to the Father: "My God, my God, why have you forsaken me?" (Mark 15:34).

Hebrews 12:2 tells us Jesus knew that beyond His trek of suffering lay a "joy," the joy of reconciling mankind to God! He relentlessly pursued that objective His whole life… a life which ended with death on a Roman cross. Despite that unwavering commitment to His mission, in a moment of deep distress, the human side of Him felt the same sense of abandonment we sometimes do in our search for understanding.

Such instances of despair are not of themselves sin. Otherwise the Bible could not have declared our Savior to be "sinless." (Hebrews 4:15) Jesus did not surrender to His despair. He endured to the finish line, committing His spirit into the hands of the very God by whom He had felt deserted in His earlier moment of consternation (Luke 23:46).

Let's look back to the example we mentioned earlier: Job. While Christ may have experienced *moments of dismay* in the midst of His life of trust in the Father, Job experienced *moments of trust* in the midst of a season of bitter laments. That may be where we too frequently find ourselves. Yet even that limited measure of faith can be a harbinger of victory.

Immediately following the previously quoted words of frustration at his inability to discover God's presence and purpose in his seemingly meaningless suffering, Job goes on to declare his trust. Job 23:10 quotes him proclaiming: "But he knows the way that I take; when he has tested me, I will come forth as gold."

This is not his only expression of faith. In chapter 19, verses 25 and 26, Job says: "I know that my Redeemer lives, and that in the end he will stand upon the earth. And after my skin has been destroyed, yet in my flesh I will see God…" Job 14:14,15 finds this prayer of expectation: "All the days of my hard service I will wait for my renewal to come. You will call and I will answer you; you will long for the creature your hands have made." In my estimation, the most remarkable statement of faith in the Lord from the lips of Job comes in chapter 13, verse 15: "Though he slay me, yet will I hope in him…"

Ultimately, God's grace and Job's measure of faith culminated in blessing. Although at the end of the story the Lord had to rebuke him for the sulky assertions of his own righteousness and wisdom, He rewards Job's faith with a new family and more wealth than he ever had before. Best of all, Job emerges from his time of testing with a greater understanding of his God.

How have you and I dealt with similar experiences? Perhaps like our canine companions we need to recognize that we were in a sense born (*again*) for the hunt. Like them, we easily celebrate the eventual capture of the object of our pursuit. But unlike them, we often fail to find joy in the journey.

Our opening Scripture for this chapter asserts that the pursuit of the things God hides is a *noble* venture... suitable to *royalty*. As children of the King of the Universe are we not *royalty*? Revelation 5:10 describes the redeemed of the earth from the Lord's perspective: "You have made them to be a kingdom and priests to serve our God, and they will reign on the earth."

It is, after all, this noble search that yields the strengthening of our faith and the deepening of our relationship with the Lord. Remember what Hebrews 11:6 tells us. God "rewards those who earnestly seek him." And recall what the Apostle Paul assures us in our godly pursuits. "...At the proper time we will reap a harvest if we do not give up" (Galatians 6:9).

Father, please sustain us during our periods of testing. Increase our passion for the hunt, and in your mercy grant us the treasures you've prepared for us.

Chapter 16:
To Fear and Not Be Afraid

Exodus 20:20 - "Do not be afraid. God has come to test you, so that the fear of God will be with you to keep you from sinning."

I'VE ALWAYS WANTED MY dogs to fear me. Yet I don't want them to be fearful. On the surface that sounds like a contradiction. It's not. Fearing me as pack leader not only enables them to please me, it enables me to more effectively look out for their best interests. On the flip side, unnecessary anxiety saps their joy.

Some of my pets have not feared me enough. Many times they've been too independent for their own good. Others have been too fearful. That robs them of much of life's pleasure. Our two Italian Greyhounds were each a prime example of those extremes.

Ranger could be so fearful that it would break your heart. His head would drop, ears go back, and his tail tuck between his legs. Then he'd begin to shiver. In some cases we knew what generated this reaction. Other times, sadly, we'd be at a loss to understand why, or to know how to appropriately comfort him.

Now, if there's such a thing as canine attention deficit disorder, Tigger was afflicted with that. It's not that he was a bad dog. His impulses were often just more powerful than his allegiance to his master. When he misbehaved, a strong word of correction would usually bring him back into line. Then ten seconds later he'd be doing the same thing. Tigger was a restless soul.

If a back yard gate was inadvertently left open, Tigger was off on an adventure... a risky behavior for a pooch whose lack of caution was not tempered by good judgment. And calling him back on those occasions was an exercise in futility. The call of the wild was stronger than his fear of the master. Inevitably I'd have to run after him and pick him up.

Thank God, those episodes never resulted in any serious injuries. But his wanderlust did scare us and him on at least one particular occasion I still recall. I'd unfolded the attic stairs and climbed up to retrieve something. A moment later, Tigger tried to follow. The resulting tumble evoked a howl that would suggest he was mortally wounded. Fortunately it left only a minor abrasion.

God has similar concerns for our good as I've had for Ranger's and Tigger's. In our key verse, He speaks through the lips of Moses to calm and instruct His people. In that passage He deals with the contrasting fears my pets have exemplified. Let's examine those two fears in the context of that scripture.

In the original Hebrew, the words "afraid" and "fear" in this passage have distinctively different meanings. The first one, where the children of Israel are told "Do not be *afraid*," addresses the common reaction of humans to someone or something that scares us. The second one, which speaks of "the *fear* of God," refers to a *reverential* kind of fear. The first is to be overcome. The second is to be cultivated.

The Lord doesn't want His people to be paralyzed by terror. Throughout the Bible we see divine words of assurance such as "fear not," or "don't be afraid." This kind of fear is a tool of the thief of souls. He uses it to break into our storehouse of trust, then attempts to steal away with its provisions. God's counter weapon for this destructive device is noted in II Timothy 1:7: "For God did not give us a spirit of timidity, but a spirit of power, of love and of self-discipline." We overcome the bad kind of fear through the powerful Spirit the Lord has imparted to us.

When the devil tries to overwhelm us with fear, we need to draw on the incomparable strength of the Holy Spirit, who's within each believer. Our trust in the power of God can turn the tide. As I John 4:4 says: "You, dear children, are from God and have overcome them [evil spirits], because the one who is in you is greater than the one who is in the world."

The enemy *wants* you to be afraid, but he *doesn't want* you to fear the Lord. Being afraid opens the door to potential loss. The fear of God opens the door to potential blessings.

What kind of blessings flow from the good kind of fear? Let's take a quick peek behind that door of divine supply. Proverbs 9:10 says "The fear of the Lord is the beginning of wisdom..." Proverbs 14:27 informs us that "The fear of the Lord is a fountain of life." And Isaiah 33:6 assures God's people that in a season of trouble "He [the Lord] will be the sure foundation for your times, a rich store of salvation and wisdom and knowledge; *the fear of the Lord is the key to this treasure.*"

The worries of life rob us of the joy of living. The reverence of the Holy One releases our divine destiny. God tells us which fear to reject and which fear to embrace, but as always He leaves the choice to us.

Tigger and Ranger had good lives with their loving masters, Carol and me, and I'm glad for that. But their days on earth could have been even richer had they wholly learned the lessons of bad fear versus good fear. By the grace of God, I hope to fully learn those lessons myself, and experience a greater measure of His love and kindness.

Chapter 17:
In Harm's Way

John 15:13 - "Greater love has no one than this,
that he lay down his life for his friends."

IT WAS A PLEASANT late summer afternoon. Carol and I were in the side yard. I'm not sure where we were headed at the time, but as usual, Tippy was accompanying us. She always wanted to be where we were.

This time her proximity led to a brush with danger. I saw the collision coming, but it was too late to totally avert it. The best I could do as Tippy suddenly crossed my path was to tumble in such a manner as to avoid landing on her. My more than two-hundred pound frame could have caused her severe, even life-ending injury.

As I scrambled to my feet, I was much relieved that I'd managed to land on the ground, not Tippy. Carol, however, rushed over to make sure I wasn't hurt. I was gratified by my wife's loving concern. Yet I realized in that moment that I'd had little thought as to my being injured. I was only worried about my beloved pet.

Now I don't fancy myself some kind of hero in this incident. Yet in retrospect, I was struck by how my sacrificial concern for Tippy's welfare was a reflection (though a pale one) of God's love toward us. Out of love, I was willing to place myself in harm's way for the sake of an inferior creature. So was Jesus.

Christ is the epitome of sacrificial love. But there was an Old Testament saint who gave us a preview of that kind of substitutionary devotion to others. His name was Moses.

Exodus chapter 32 recounts the story of Israel's great sin of idolatry, and the Lord's subsequent anger. In reaction to God's judgment, Moses entered, as he would many times during his ministry, into the role of intercessor. He confessed what a terrible sin his people had committed, and pleaded for forgiveness for them. Then he uttered words that never cease to astound me: "…but if not, then blot me out of the book you have written" (Exodus 32:32). Moses was willing to have his name removed from God's book of life… to be consigned to hell… so that his brothers and sisters could be forgiven!

In Deuteronomy 18:15 Moses predicted: "The Lord your God will raise up for you a prophet like me from among your own brothers. You must listen to him." In both Acts 3:22 and 7:37, Scripture confirms that Moses was pointing ahead to the Messiah, Jesus of Nazareth.

Jesus is the greatest intercessor of all time. He prayed fervently for us during His earthly ministry. Since His ascension into heaven two-thousand years ago, until this very day, Christ stands at the right hand of the Father in Heaven interceding for you and me (Romans 8:34). But His role as intercessor carried him beyond the ministry of prayer. It led Him to the place of death!

Numerous men and women have given their lives for others over the centuries. The Lord offered high praise for their sacrifice, proclaiming that such an act demonstrates the highest kind of love. But only Jesus bore the penalty for *all* the sins of *all* mankind. His death alone accomplished redemption for everyone who surrenders to Him in faith… "once for all" (Hebrews 10:10).

No one ever suffered the cruel death that belonged to Jesus alone. Although crucifixion was one of the most excruciating forms of execution ever devised, it was not that awful method which made His death so uniquely painful. It was the weight of every sin that ever has been and ever will be committed by fallen human beings. That was a horror that tore at the very fabric of His sinless soul. It was a terror that reached its climax when he cried out in indescribable agony: "My God, my God, why have you forsaken me?" (Mark 15:34).

55

All other sacrificial deaths, noble as they may be, pale in comparison. So do all other loves. We're afforded a glimpse of *Christ's* love for us in the accounts of His crucifixion in the Gospels. But what of *God the Father's* love? We know He's the one who loved us enough to send His Son in the first place (John 3:16). Still, the curtain of Heaven was not pulled back to reveal the anguish the Father endured as He had to turn His back on the Savior who hung on a cross between Heaven and earth... the beloved Son in Whom He was "well-pleased."

This unparalleled love was directed toward inferior creatures who'd rejected their Creator's rightful and kindly authority. The Apostle Paul reminds us in Romans 5:8: "But God demonstrates his own love for us in this: While we were still sinners, Christ died for us." Then in Romans 8:32 he rejoices in the scope of this divine love. "He who did not spare his own Son, but gave him up for us all—how will he not also, along with him, graciously give us *all* things?"

My awkward tumble, risking injury to myself in order to spare my dear Tippy, was no grand sacrifice. But it was a reflection of God's love for us... a love He wants us to extend to others. "This is how we know what love is: Jesus Christ laid down his life for us. And we ought to lay down our lives for our brothers" (I John 3:16).

Are we willing to follow His example and place ourselves in harm's way... not necessarily physically, but perhaps emotionally, socially, economically, etc... for our friends? Father, please make us more like Your Son and our Elder Brother, Jesus.

Chapter 18:
Why Do I Put Up with This?

I Peter 4:8 - "...because love covers over a multitude of sins."

IT HAD HAPPENED ON occasion before. This time though, my frustration peaked. I arrived home weary and wanting to relax after a hard day's work. I let Tigger and Ranger out of their crates only to discover that Ranger had once again pooped in his. I scolded him and carted his soiled crate outside. I would have to launder his blanket, take his crate apart and scrub it down, allow it to dry, reassemble it, then drag it back into the house and re-line it with the now clean blanket!

Exasperated, I asked myself, "Why do I put up with this?" Without a millisecond of hesitation the answer echoed in my heart: "Because I love this little creature." It was true. Ranger's misbehavior could upset me, but it could never destroy my affection for him. The *spiritual* parallel to this *natural* experience did not escape me. God had repeatedly put up with my smelly messes over the years, simply because He loved me.

Ever feel like the Lord can't possibly love you because of your failures, especially those you seem to repeat? You'd be amazed to find out how many other Christians struggle with those same thoughts. I've rubbed elbows with countless of my fellow believers over the last half century, many of them godly ministers and pillars of the church. I have yet to meet a single one without sin. And all have wrestled at one time or another with feelings of inadequacy and unworthiness.

Do our shortcomings disappoint God? Do they now and then even anger Him? The answer is obvious: of course! God is holy and He hates sin.

Let me ask another question whose answer may seem apparent as well. What is sin, anyway? We have a pretty good idea what it is. We may define sin by offering examples: theft, murder, adultery... you know, the *really bad* things. Or maybe we take a broader approach and characterize sin as simply disobeying *any* command of God. Both of these answers bear the signature of truth. But they fail to get to the heart of the matter.

Both the Hebrew (Old Testament) and Greek (New Testament) words for sin have as their root meaning the concept of "missing the mark..." or *missing the target*, so to speak. You see, God has an ideal for all of His children: *perfection*. Adam and Eve possessed perfection through innocence. That is, they did until they fell into Satan's trap. Jesus was perfect through total submission and obedience to the Father, and He never stumbled. That perfection qualified Jesus to be the only man who could ever bear the punishment for the sins of the whole world.

Now, if sin is *missing* the mark, then perfection is *hitting* the mark. But perfection is not simply an end in itself. It affords us all the blessings that the Lord originally intended for mankind to enjoy. Chief among those blessings is an unencumbered relationship with our Creator. That's the greatest joy in life. And that sweet relationship with God is the mark of which sin falls short. For that reason above all others, sin angers God. Sin comes between Him and the beings He created to have loving fellowship with for eternity.

Psalm 103:13,14 broadcasts good news for sinners. "As a father has compassion on his children, so the Lord has compassion on those who fear him; for he knows how we are formed, he remembers that we are dust." In His compassion for us, God provided a means to restore our broken relationship. "...God was reconciling the world to himself in Christ, not counting men's sins against them" (II Corinthians 5:19).

Jesus, the perfect substitute for sinners, carved with His own nail-scarred hands the channel through which the river of God's compassion can flow into our lives. Christ's sacrifice on the cross made it possible for the Father to satisfy His holy demand for sin's awful penalty, and at the same time direct His kindness to the imperfect. That wondrous transaction enables God to reach past the wretched stench of our fallen humanity to touch us with His unremitting love, love that redeems our souls from Hell and sets us on the road to Heaven.

Then the Lord provides the spiritual mirror known as the Bible to help us see how we stumble along the path, and how we can rise again. In the first chapter of James, the Apostle lays it out for us. "Anyone who listens to the word but does not do what it says is like a man who looks at his face in a mirror and, after looking at himself, goes away and immediately forgets what he looks like. But the man who looks intently into the perfect law that gives freedom, and continues to do this, not forgetting what he has heard, but doing it—he will be blessed in what he does" (verses 22-25).

This process is called *sanctification*. It means to be "set apart," in this case set apart *unto God*. In the closing days of His earthly life Jesus prayed for the Father to accomplish this transformational work in us. "Sanctify them by the truth; your word is truth" (John 17:17). Sanctification is an ongoing challenge for every believer.

When we fall short, as we inevitably will sometimes, we're never cut off from the love of God. As cited above, in chapter 1 of his divinely inspired letter, James does insist that we must not settle for less than the pursuit of godly perfection. But in chapter 2 he trumpets the power of God's mercy when we stumble in our pursuit. "Mercy triumphs over judgment!" (verse 13).

Are you wallowing in your own waste? Perhaps you've tried to hide your sin under the blanket. Don't cover the mess and don't despair. Confess your sin to the Lord and receive His mercy. Far more than Ranger, you have a Master who loves you in spite of your mess. His love will reach past your failures and deal with what you never properly can on your own. Remember, "…love covers over a multitude of sins."

Chapter 19:
My Friends

James 2:23 - "...and he was called God's friend."

FAMILY AND FRIENDS... WHEN it comes to life's relationships those are the two dominant words. But can we include pet dogs in that special circle? Generally speaking, friends and family are of the *Homo sapiens* variety. Whether *Canis lupus familiaris* can truly be our friends might depend on your definition of the word.

The American Heritage Dictionary's number one meaning for friend is: "a person whom one knows, likes, and trusts." The word *person* would seem to exclude animals. However, the Merriam-Webster Dictionary's primary definition is as follows: "one attached to another by affection or esteem." Bingo! That works for me! Now, I could get into a discussion about the definitions of *one* and *another,* but I'll leave that challenge to someone else. For now I'm content to believe those words apply to *Canis lupus familiaris* as well as *Homo sapiens.*

There's no question that I've considered my dogs friends... maybe even family. In spite of the fact that their level of intelligence is far below mine (though some may argue that point), I count them among my friends. My hounds and I are "attached... by affection or esteem." On occasion I even address one of them directly as "my friend," or "my little buddy." I believe their friendship is a gift from the Lord to me.

Others of my fellowmen may consider that amazing... perhaps even downright strange. Yet how much more amazing and strange is it that a mere human being would be called a friend of Almighty God?

Friendship, of course, should be a two-way street. And for a self-existent, sovereign God, that means not only befriending an inferior created being, but reaching past his obnoxious behavior. The Lord has been doing just that since sin entered and destroyed the paradise He originally designed as the happy home of humans. Friendship between God and man has always been initiated by Him.

The Bible communicates God's loving outreach to mankind in one form or another from cover to cover. The clearest demonstration of that amazing friendship, however, is offered in the life and death of His Son, Jesus. A particularly striking example of this is found in Luke 7:34. There Christ is accused by His enemies of being a friend of tax collectors (generally considered a corrupt and dishonest lot in those days) and "sinners." Though intended as a condemnation, this demeaning accusation pointed to a wonderful fact: Jesus *was* and *is* a friend to sinners!

To me, however, the most astonishing extension of the Lord's hand of friendship happened in the hours just before His crucifixion, when Judas Iscariot arrived with a large armed mob to betray Him. In Matthew 26:50 we witness Jesus, knowing exactly what was going on, addressing His chosen apostle-turned-traitor as "Friend." Amazing!

"Judas" has since become a synonym for "traitor." How sad. Understand, though, that the tragedy of his life was not the result of God's animosity, or even indifference, toward Judas. It was the outcome of a lifestyle of choosing earthly wealth over a rich eternal relationship with the Lord. As we previously pointed out, friendship should be a two-way street.

In the Bible verse we used as a springboard for this discussion, Abraham is identified as "God's friend." As we learned from the story of Judas, not everyone accepts the offer of divine friendship. And not all who choose to be a friend of the Lord enjoy the same level of intimacy. This is not to suggest that Abraham was perfect. He clearly was not. But something was at the root of his exceptional status.

The late Bible teacher and author, Judson Cornwall, once called my attention to a quite revealing feature of God's Word. He pointed out that there are many people whose names appear in Scripture. We're given little information about most of them. But when we come across the name of one who had a real heart quest for God, the account of their life usually generates details. Those details indicate the value the Lord places on such special friendships, and offer insights we can use in our personal pursuit of intimacy with Him.

The simple formula for developing one of those close relationships with God is set forth in James 4:8. "Come near to God and he will come near to you." Let's step back into the world of canines again and see if the parallel holds up. All of my dogs have been my friends. But the bond with some of them has been closer than with others. What makes the difference? ...their pursuit of me.

Some of my pets were more individualistic. They were somewhat attached to me, but other pursuits often took precedence. Others valued their relationship with me more highly. Pleasing me was a priority. Spending time with me was paramount. They faithfully followed me from place to place whenever I moved about. I've loved them all. But a few have been considered *special* friends because they made it plain how much they wanted to be near me.

Jesus had a large number of followers during His earthly ministry. Not all were as close to Him as some who seemed to be afforded unusual proximity. Seventy-two were set apart for an honored ministry as advance representatives of Christ (Luke 10:1). Twelve were appointed to be His companions and share preaching responsibilities (Mark 3:14). Three were exclusively invited to a few uniquely intimate events with their Master (Matthew 17:1). And one, who was referred to as "the disciple whom Jesus loved" (John 13:23), reclined nearest Jesus at the Last Supper.

How close a friendship with the Lord do you want? He's already expressed His desire toward you. Now He longs for you to reciprocate. Describing those who passionately pursue the Lord, preacher and author Tommy Tenney coined the phrase "God chasers." I want to be part of that kind of fraternity. Do you?

Chapter 20:
The Master Chef

John 4:32 - "…I have food to eat that you know nothing about."

HAVE YOU EVER NOTICED how our hounds somehow inherently know that human food is better than dog food? No one has to tell them. That knowledge seems to be instinctive. They'll abandon their regular diet in a moment for a chance to relish even a smidgen of people food.

Over the years my wife and I have minimized the amount of table scraps we give our dogs. But that hasn't kept them from the frenzied delight they take in those people food treats that have been doled out. Of course, they have their favorites. Among them are meat and cheese. And in more recent years our Italian Greyhound stable-mates Tigger and Ranger discovered a passion for fruit smoothies. That's right! Those healthy milk shake alternatives trigger acute canine drooling.

God's faithful servants likewise have an innate awareness that the Master has things on His menu which would make the finest restaurant cuisine seem like dumpster fare by comparison. It's not that we disdain the food He's provided for the pleasure of our senses and the health of our bodies. It's that at our core… in our eternal spirits… we crave a higher satisfaction than that afforded by anything that passes from our mouths to our bellies.

Jesus illustrated this dimension of spiritual hunger to His disciples in the gospel story referenced above. In John chapter 4 we read how He passed through Samaria. There at Jacob's well He revealed Himself as the promised Messiah to an inquisitive, wayward woman. His disciples had gone into town to buy food, and when they returned and found Christ talking with that woman they were both surprised and concerned.

Their surprise was because Jesus was talking to a woman… and a Samaritan woman at that! You see, in those days it was considered more than a little improper for a man (particularly a Rabbi) to speak to a woman in public. To make things worse, this female was Samaritan. Samaritans were of mixed race, part Jew and part Gentile, and a centuries old hatred lingered between Jews and Samaritans.

Jesus never stood on the traditions of men. He was on a mission from God, the Father. No cultural prohibition would be allowed to stand in the way. This Samaritan woman was a thirsty soul, and Jesus was sent from heaven to bring water from the well of salvation to her and others like her. He led her to faith in Himself, and through her witness, her home town experienced a revival!

The whole thing may have surprised Jesus' disciples, but it was no shock to His Father. God had ordained this encounter, and Christ had followed His Father's plan in complete obedience.

The disciples' surprise at discovering the Master talking to a woman was not expressed out loud, but their concern for Jesus physical well-being was. They urged Him, "Rabbi, eat something." His response raised even more questions for these twelve men still on the learning curve. As quoted at the head of this chapter, He said: "I have food to eat that you know nothing about." They were puzzled, and wondered among themselves if someone had somehow gotten a meal to Jesus before they'd arrived.

The Master explained: "My food is to do the will of him who sent me and to finish his work." The context offers no indication as to whether the disciples grasped the full meaning of Jesus' words in that moment. Still, I have no doubt that they ultimately learned the lesson and caught the hunger. Their later lives make it evident. To adapt a beloved phrase from the writings of Irish poet Thomas Moore, " Earth hath no *cuisine* Heaven cannot *surpass*."

Christ understood this truth before He even began His ministry. Prior to preaching any sermon, Jesus spent forty days alone in the desert without the nourishment or pleasure of a single crumb of food. Later He would share many earthly feasts with others. But during that season He was seeking a greater satisfaction from a purer diet. He was preparing His spirit to dine at the table of the Father's glorious plan for the salvation of mankind.

In the fourth chapter of Matthew we observe Satan tempting Jesus at the close of this forty day fast. The tempter challenged Him to use His divine authority to gratify His own fleshly hunger. Jesus spurned that lure and rebuked the devil. "It is written: 'Man does not live on bread alone, but on every word that comes from the mouth of God'" (verse 4).

In the very next chapter, Matthew records Christ's first public message. We've come to know it as *The Sermon on the Mount*. In it the Lord pronounces one of my favorite promises in all of Scripture: "Blessed are those who hunger and thirst for righteousness, for they will be filled" (verse 6).

There's no need to spurn the *physical* food the benevolent Creator has provided for us... except for seasons of fasting and prayer. But we need to keep our sights high, and take advantage of every opportunity to enjoy the *spiritual* food He gives to those of His servants who faithfully do His bidding. No spread on the planet can compare to the banquet awaiting us at each visit to our Heavenly Father's table.

Chapter 21:
Wild or Domestic?

Exodus 32:25 - "...running wild and ...out of control..."

AN EPISODE OF THE 1970's television series "The Waltons" featured a dilemma faced by the middle daughter of the clan, Erin. She adopts a rescued fawn, but is forced by law to surrender it to the local game warden. She's given two options: the warden can return it to the forest, or place it in a wildlife preserve. In the forest it'll live with the risks and rewards of its natural habitat. In the preserve it'll be watched over and protected. Eventually, Erin opts to have it released back into the wild, a choice most naturalists would applaud.

Many naturalists virtually worship nature, cruel as it may often be. Unfortunately they don't recognize that *current* nature is *fallen* nature. It retains a level of its original beauty and harmony, but it's terribly flawed. The question is: which came first, wild animals or domestic ones? Most naturalists would insist that wild creatures came first, and that humans later domesticated certain kinds of animals. I'm convinced they're wrong, and that the opening chapters of Genesis hold the real answer.

There we learn that in earth's beginning none of the animals faced the kinds of hazards today's wild creatures do. All were herbivores. That is, they ate only plants, not other animals. There were no predators and prey. The Lord saw to it that all were lovingly cared for by Himself and His representatives: human beings. But the curse of sin fell upon all creation and everything changed.

My favorite species of the many fascinating animals God made, dogs, fall into two main categories: wild and domestic. Both types

66

are the same species and can interbreed. They share common traits, but their lifestyles are very different.

In every previous chapter of this book I've dealt exclusively with domestic dogs. In the spiritual analogies offered they represent Christians. Imperfect though they may be at times, believers, as with pet dogs, are still in the Master's care. In this final chapter though, wild dogs become part of our allegory. They represent souls not surrendered to any master except their own tainted appetites and instincts.

Wolves, coyotes, foxes, and other wild canines in large part run free. Most of them live in social structures among their own kind, in units known as packs. While they enjoy a level of intra-breed affection, they miss out on the love and watchful care of loving humans from which their domestic counterparts benefit. The competition for alpha male and female leaders takes its toll both physically and emotionally. They live by the code of kill or be killed. They're subject to the prospect of starvation. That's part of the price for that kind of freedom in the wild.

On the other hand, pet dogs do have restrictions on their activities. They're usually confined to a home, a fenced yard, or by a leash. These restrictions, however, contribute to their safety and well-being. They enjoy the love and provision of devoted masters. The ongoing brawls over the position of top dog, with all the intrinsic penalties, are minimized or eliminated. There's no need to hunt for food or face starvation.

Grant you, there are neglectful and even cruel dog owners. But thankfully they're the exception, and those people are not representative of a loving heavenly Master. In Proverbs 12:10 God calls that kind of owner *wicked*. "A righteous man cares for the needs of his animal, but the kindest acts of the wicked are cruel."

Perhaps drawing from the perspective of prevailing naturalistic evolutionary philosophy, Western culture largely glorifies the *wild* lifestyle for people, too. Songs like "Born to Be Wild" from the 1960's, and movies like "Wild Things" from the 1990's, are representative of the mentality that's helped steer much of our nation's morals into the realm of base animal passions.

That's what happened to the people of Israel in the Bible passage that launches this chapter. They chose to create and worship a golden calf. Their pagan worship quickly collapsed into a drunken orgy.

Fast forward to twenty-first century America. For many here, freedom has become a synonym for things like selfish greed, gratuitous violence and promiscuous sex. We choose to descend into the corrupt aspects of fallen nature rather than rise to the heights of the new nature offered through the Gospel of Christ.

But one doesn't have to exhibit such blatant immorality to live like wild creatures. We can simply say to our Creator: "I won't let You tell me what to do. I'm going to live *my* life *my* way!" That's what our original ancestors Adam and Eve did, and ever since, every person on the planet (with One notable exception) has been born into this rebellion against God. In Psalm 51:5 Israel's King David put it like this: "Surely I was sinful at birth, sinful from the time my mother conceived me."

Now, wolves and other wild dogs risk much more danger in life than their domestic counterparts. But no canine risks an eternity in Hell. That potential fate remains the exclusive domain of human beings who reject their Creator's legitimate claims. So if you choose to live life estranged from God, you not only lose the blessings of His love and care on Earth, you'll spend forever paying for the sins for which Jesus already died.

The decision is yours. There is a wonderful means of escape from sin and its consequences. It comes through the aforementioned substitutionary death of Jesus Christ. He suffered the penalty for your sins and mine. Then He rose from the dead three days later to grant us victory over the grave as part of the deal. So after passing from this life we go to a place of inconceivable joy to spend forever with the One Who loves us with an incomprehendable love.

Will you have to give up your prized autonomy to gain this eternal benefit? Will there be boundaries on your behavior? Absolutely! But the appeal of self-rule is an illusion, and those restraining borders you're inclined to loathe were instituted in God's Word for your good. You gain a wonderful relationship with the Lord in this life, plus an even better one in the life to come. What do you choose? ...

the wild life or the domesticated one? ...to believe the Devil's lies or God's truth?

Confess to God in this moment that you're a sinner. Tell Him you want to change but you can't do it yourself. Believe that Jesus was the Son of God who died for you and rose from the dead. Ask for His forgiveness. Tell him you'll live for Him from now on. I made that decision many years ago and I don't regret it. Neither will you.

About the Author

Sam Mason brings a lifetime of Christian experience and decades of dog ownership to bear on the contents of Talking Dogs.

Growing up in a Christian home in western Pennsylvania, he committed his life to the Lord at an early age. He began public ministry at 13, singing and speaking over the next 4 years with a gospel quartet at roughly 150 church services, concerts, and other events throughout the state. Upon high school graduation he attended Zion Bible Institute (now Zion Bible College) in New England, where he met his wife, Carol. He graduated as class valedictorian in 1970, and he and Carol were married several months later. They have three children: Kim (now deceased), Nicole, and Matt, and several grandchildren. The couple currently live in Virginia.

Sam is an avid student of Scripture and has spent virtually all of his adult career in ministry. He's been a pastor, teacher, evangelist, singer, and Christian broadcaster. He's served on the boards of local, regional, and international ministries. Sam is a published songwriter and book author. His first book, **The Curse**, deals with the far reaching effects of the ubiquitous curse that resulted from original sin, and how God's plan has always been for blessing instead. He's been gratified by people who report discovering a greater understanding of life on this planet, some even experiencing a transformational encounter with God, as a result of reading **The Curse**.

Sam has had a love affair with dogs since boyhood, and has experienced the sublime pleasure of loving canine relationships throughout his adult life. He's been an enthusiastic student and observer of dog behavior during these years of pet ownership. He hopes you'll now benefit from the spiritual insights he's gained through the inspiration the Lord shared with him via his "special" friends.

Made in the USA
Columbia, SC
27 November 2019

CONTENTS